Jesus of Nazareth

JESUS OF NAZARETH

I. HIS PERSONAL CHARACTER.
II. HIS ETHICAL TEACHINGS.
III. HIS SUPERNATURAL WORKS.

THREE LECTURES BEFORE THE Y. M. C. A. OF JOHNS HOPKINS UNIVERSITY, IN LEVERING HALL.

JOHN A. BROADUS, D.D., LL.D.,
President of the Southern Baptist Theological Seminary.

Solid Ground Christian Books
Birmingham, Alabama USA

Solid Ground Christian Books
2090 Columbiana Rd, Suite 2000
Birmingham, AL 35216
205-443-0311
sgcb@charter.net
http://solid-ground-books.com

Jesus of Nazareth
HIS CHARACTER, HIS TEACHINGS, AND HIS SUPERNATURAL WORKS

John Albert Broadus (1827-1895)

Taken from 1890 edition by A.C. Armstrong & Son, New York

Solid Ground Classic Reprints

First printing of new edition June 2005

Cover work by Borgo Design, Tuscaloosa, AL
Contact them at nelbrown@comcast.net

ISBN: 1-932474-89-7

PREFACE.

These lectures were delivered in March, 1890, at the instance of Eugene Levering, Esq., of Baltimore, in the Hall which he has recently erected and given to the Johns Hopkins University, for the use of the Young Men's Christian Association of that institution; and the President of the Y. M. C. A. specially requested their publication. They were not designed as class-room lectures, since many not connected with the University were invited to attend.

The subject treated seems to possess an ever-deepening interest at the present time. The personal character of Jesus is now widely perceived to be an important guarantee of his teachings and works. This character is presented by the first lecture in a way that to some may appear lacking in devout warmth; but the object was to gain the

3

concurrence of every person who will calmly survey the historical facts, and thus to lay a foundation for what would follow. It is hoped that the second lecture will tend to rectify certain erroneous but quite prevalent views of the Saviour's teaching; and that the third lecture may be found to have some argumentative force in regard to his mission and claims.

The little volume is the fruit of life-time studies, and has been prepared with the author's best exertions, and a great desire to promote "the knowledge of Jesus, the most excellent of the sciences."

J. A. B.

LOUISVILLE, KY.,
May, 1890.

CONTENTS.

I.

The Personal Character of Jesus.

THE PERSONAL CHARACTER OF JESUS.

WHATEVER else many of us believe as to
Jesus the Saviour, all men believe in his
thorough humanity. The orthodox world has often
failed to make full *practical* recognition of his humanity, through an exclusive attention to other
views of his person and work ; and the modern historical spirit has been a benefactor to orthodoxy by
bringing out his human character and life as a vivid
reality. Jesus of Nazareth, the Founder of Christianity, stands before us to-day as one of the defi-
nite personages of human history. The leading
facts of his career, the chief peculiarities of his
teaching, the distinctive traits of his character, are
now really beyond dispute. And the *excellence* of
his character, its high and peerless excellence, is
now recognized not only by Christians of every
type and by many Jews, but by persons holding
almost every form of unbelief. Time was, even in
the modern centuries, when some men of talents
and culture reviled him as an impostor or a fanatic,
as did some of the blinded Jews who were his contemporaries. But there is hardly a man in all
the world who would speak thus to-day. Even
persons who allow themselves to ridicule the Bible,

and the God whom it describes, are unwilling now to speak lightly of Jesus; and if in some rare cases a man attempts to hint possible and slight defect, he seems to do so with reluctance, and turns quickly away to join the chorus of eulogy. Robert Browning, in a letter published since his death, cites several utterances of men of genius as to the Christian faith, and among them one from Charles Lamb. "In a gay fancy with some friends, as to how he and they would feel if the greatest of the dead were to appear suddenly in flesh and blood once more—on the final suggestion, 'And if Christ entered this room?' he changed his manner at once and stuttered out, as his manner was when moved, 'You see, if Shakespeare entered we should all rise; if *he* appeared, we must kneel.'" Such reverence is not a mere result of Christian education, of Christian literature and art and usages; it will be felt by any person of susceptible nature who will thoughtfully read one of the gospels at a single sitting, and alone with his beating heart and his God.

Of a character thus unique, unparalleled, universally reverenced, how can we attempt a portraiture? The effort is fore-doomed to failure. It must be disappointing to taste and unsatisfying to devotion. No painter among all the great names has made a picture of Jesus which a loving reader of the gospels can feel to be adequate. How can we depict his character in words? But if one undertakes the task, of all things he must beware of high-wrought expressions. The most inadequate language is less unworthy of Jesus than inflated language. And it may contribute towards the design of these lectures if we attempt, in sheer simplicity, to bring before our minds the circumstances of his self-manifestation, and the more easily apprehended traits of his character. The present sketch has been wrought out from the gospels themselves, with suggestions afterwards welcomed from several recent writings. For the present we must leave almost entirely out of view the Saviour's beautiful teachings and glorious works, which are to be considered on other occasions.

Notice first the *external conditions* of his life. We all know that he was reared in a small and obscure village, whose inhabitants were rude and violent, and had an ill-name among their neighbors. Not once nor twice only have the world's wisest and greatest, the world's teachers and rulers, sprung from some petty village or country neighborhood. We know that Jesus was reared in poverty, and was himself a mechanic, a worker in wood. Justin Martyr, who lived a hundred years later in the same region, states the tradition that he made ploughs and ox-yokes. It ought to be clearly brought out in our time that the Founder of Christianity spent his early life as what we call a working-man. Yet remember that from boyhood he went at least once a year, and probably oftener, to the great city of Jerusalem, making the journey amid scenes of varied natural beauty and all manner of sacred associations, to mingle with vast crowds from every district of the Holy Land and from many a distant country, and to take part in impressive religious ceremonies, to join in chanting the sweet Psalms of David, and listen long to

the fervent reading of ancient record and high prophetic instruction and exhortation. It is difficult to
estimate the benefits that would be derived by a
highly impressible youthful nature during the whole
period between the age of twelve and that of thirty,
from such journeys and weeks of abiding in the
Holy City.

During his public ministry he had no home, and
spent most of his time in travelling, on foot, busy
with public and private teaching, and sustained by
the hospitality of friends and sometimes of stran-
gers, or by money contributed by generous women
for the support of himself and his followers. Yet
observe that he did not do this as meritorious
asceticism, but simply from a desire to spend his
whole time in doing good, throughout a ministry
which he foresaw must be short. Even among
ourselves there are men so devoted to science or
art, to authorship or teaching or religious ministra-
tions, that they often share the feeling of the great
scientific man who said, "I haven't time to make
money." This early life was very different from
that of Sakhya Muni, the Founder of Buddhism,
who is represented as the son of a wealthy king,
dwelling for years in a home of luxury, and leaving
it to become an ascetic. Jesus showed no tinge of
asceticism. John the forerunner made his life an
object lesson to a luxurious age, as Elijah had done
long before, by dwelling for years among the wild
hills, with the garb and the food of the poorest.
But it was quite otherwise with Jesus. He wore
good clothing, for we read of a tunic woven without
seam, which at that day must have been a costly

garment. He spent days at a wedding feast, which the forerunner would probably not have consented to attend. He accepted invitations from the rich, and conformed to social usage by reclining on a couch beside the table in the luxurious Persian fashion; and, as he himself expressly mentions, ate and drank what others did, though it exposed him even then to misconception and unkind remark. Jesus touched life at many points, yet it was mainly and essentially the life of the poor. The profound literary and artistic interest now felt in the life of the poor, as dealing with what is "common to man," ought to awaken sympathy with the Beginnings of Christianity.

Quietly pursuing the healthy duties of an humble calling, profoundly pondering from boyhood the prophetic writings, Jesus patiently waited till the time came for him to appear and act. The earliest period at which a man was then supposed to be mature enough for highly responsible functions was something like the age of thirty. At that age the Saviour came forth without delay, and after a ministry of not more than three or four years he left the earth. He taught and died a young man. To all the other great achievements of young men must be added this incomparable fact, that a young man gave us Christianity.

Consider next the *personal religious life* of Jesus. It is remarkable how often we find mention of his *praying.* The innocent and holy One gave frequent recognition of dependence on God, which is one of the chief elements of religious feeling and conviction. If any human being was ever able to stand alone in the universe, without leaning on God, it might have been true of him. Not the guilty alone, nor the perilously weak, have occasion to lift the heart in prayer. Jesus habitually and lovingly prayed. Nor did he merely keep up the habit of stated devotion, but he made special prayer upon various recorded occasions. At his baptism we are told that he was praying, and also on the Mount of Transfiguration. He spent a night in prayer when about to select the Twelve. They were to be the companions of his remaining life, and the responsible messengers of his teaching after that life should be ended. The selection was therefore immensely important, and he made it after protracted and special prayer. When the fanatical multitude of five thousand vehemently declared that they would make him *king* even against his will, and all his patient spiritual instructions seemed to have gone for nothing, he bade them depart and went up into the mountain to pray. Thrice in Gethsemane he withdrew to agonize in prayer, and his last words on the cross were words of prayer. Strange that heedless, bustling, self-sufficient humanity does not see its own folly when contemplating that life of prayer.

Remarkable *familiarity with the sacred writings* appears already in the glimpse we catch of Jesus at the age of twelve years, and comes out in his constant use of Scripture for argument and instruction throughout his ministry. He also used it for his personal support in times of special trial. In the strange and wonderful scene of manifested temptation, he three times quotes the book of Deuteronomy as an answer to the tempter, and on the cross three times quotes the Psalms.

Jesus habitually attended upon *public worship* in the synagogues. He must have been often pained or repelled by wrong explanations of the sacred writings, by the repetition of foolish traditions, by unwise counsel and exhortation, but we are expressly told that it was "his custom" to go into the synagogue. How little did the men who spoke imagine the thoughts revolving in the mind of a quiet youth in the assembly; even as we now little know the slowly-developing wisdom, the latent potencies of some student to whom we lecture, some child to whom we preach.* Jesus also went regularly, as we have already seen, to the great religious festivals at the temple.

From the means contributed to the support of himself and his followers he was accustomed to give something to the poor. Thus when Judas went out from the last paschal supper, after the Master had said, "What thou doest, do quickly," some of the disciples thought it meant that he should give to the poor. The Saviour once declared that "it is more blessed to give than to receive." In spiritual things he and his apostles were constantly the givers; but even in temporal things, where it was their part to receive, they must not be denied some share in the higher happiness of giving.

In every way Jesus radiated forth an atmosphere of goodness; he presented the beauty of holiness in living incarnation. We can see that to be near him

---

* Compare Stalker, "Imago Christi."

often awakened in men the feeling that God was
near. It is so now. Many shrink from reading
the gospels attentively because getting near to
Jesus makes holiness seem so real, and renders
their own sinfulness a matter of painful consciousness.

Yet this great Teacher of spiritual truth, and
model of public worship and private devotion, was
constantly manifesting a deep interest in Nature,
and in the outward life of men. He watched the
dark, violet-colored lily of Galilee, recalling the
purple robes of Solomon in all his glory, and the
minute mustard-seed which grew into so large a
plant. He saw with interest the little sparrow fly-
ing or falling to the ground, and the eagles swoop-
ing down from a distance upon their proper food.
He loved retirement to some mountain top. In the
last summer of the Galilean ministry he kept withdrawing from Capernaum, in the deep and heated
caldron of the Lake of Galilee, far below the level
of the Mediterranean, to mountain regions in every
direction. No one can climb the high hill west of
Nazareth without fancying that often, when the
day's work was done, the young carpenter climbed
to that summit, gazing with delight upon the blue
Mediterranean, then in another direction upon the
snow-clad range of Mount Lebanon, and far and
wide over the Holy Land.

He was also a close observer of ordinary human
pursuits. He drew illustration in his teaching
from patching clothes, and bottling wine, and sow-
ing wheat, and reaping when the stalks were white
for the harvest, and from boys at play. Some

great painter ought to have given us that scene, children sitting in the market-place engaged in their sports, while Jesus stood by and looked with kindly face upon them. He dearly loved little children, and they for their part would leap from their mothers' arms into his arms. He was deeply interested in human *enjoyments*. He not only attended the wedding feast at Cana, but practically ministered to the gratification of the guests and aided the bridegroom in hospitality. When reclining at the tables of the rich, at feasts made in his honor, he was not silent nor severe, but conversed with the company, and introduced religious lessons suggested by the circumstances. It is indeed remarkable, as some one has observed, how many of his most striking sayings are literally " table-talk." *

Look now at the *private relations* of Jesus, concerning which we are not without interesting points of information. As a child of twelve years, on his first visit to Jerusalem, he was found in one of the theological colleges, sitting in the midst of the rabbinical professors, listening intently and eagerly questioning ; and all present were amazed, not simply at his questions, for many a child asks wonderful questions, but " at his understanding and his answers." He expressed surprise that Joseph and Mary should not know where to find him, for of course he ought to be in his Father's house, at the temple. He really was, in some respects, what many boys imagine they are, wiser than his par-

* Stalker.

ents ; and yet, as an obedient child, he left that scene
of delightful studies and went back with them to
Nazareth, and was subject unto them.   This filial
subjection doubtless continued until his public
ministry began.   At the wedding of Cana he intimated to his mother that she must not now seek
to control his actions.   The language employed is
not unkind, as some think it in our version.   For
the term "woman" was also employed by him
when speaking to her upon the cross ; and the
phrase rendered "what have I to do with thee ?"
means rather, what have we in common ?—a not unkind suggestion that he had now entered upon
duties which she must not attempt to control.   One
of the well-known Latin hymns of the great me-
diæval period gives a most pathetic picture of the
mother of Jesus standing sad and tearful beside his
cross.   The Saviour was dying, a young man ; and
beholding his widowed mother, he felt, amid all his
strange sufferings, the loving impulse with which
every young man can sympathize, to make some
provision for her earthly future.   He had a faithful
friend standing by, the friend of his bosom, known
among all the rest as one peculiarly loved.   This
friend was not destitute, but had a home of his
own; and to him the dying Teacher commended his
mother, that henceforth *they* should be mother and
son.   The simple words possess for all earth's sons
and all earth's mothers an unspeakable pathos.

We have just been reminded that certain of his
followers appear as in a peculiar sense the *friends*
of Jesus.   So it is expressly stated that "Jesus
loved Martha, and her sister, and Lazarus."   We

can see that the Twelve and some other friends were *familiar* with him, freely offering counsel and even making complaint. The ardent Peter, when told more than six months in advance that the Master was going to Jerusalem and would there be crucified, eagerly remonstrated: "Be it far from thee, Lord; this shall never be unto thee." When the loving family at Bethany first appear in the history Martha says, "Lord, carest thou not that my sister hath left me to serve alone?" implying that he ought to care. When he heard of Lazarus' sickness, and after two days' delay proposed a return to Judea, the disciples *objected*, saying that the Jews in Jerusalem had recently sought to stone him, and it was imprudent to go thither again. When he arrived at Bethany, and the two sisters met him separately, each of them said in a complaining tone, "Lord, if thou hadst been *here*, my brother had not died." These expressions show that he admitted his friends to the closest intimacy. Great as was the reverence awakened by his character and teachings and works, they did not exclude the familiarity of friendship. And we ought to note how exactly Jesus suited himself to the disposition of his friends; as for example on meeting the sorrowing sisters at Bethany, he reasoned with the active and energetic Martha, and with the gentle, contemplative Mary he wept in silent sympathy. At the crisis of agony in Gethsemane he wished to have near him the three most cherished friends among his followers; as any one in a season of great suffering desires to be much alone, and yet to have dear friends close by.

This great instructor of mankind was a notable *Teacher of teachers.* The twelve disciples were subjected to a very careful and protracted training. We can discern the successive stages. He first called one and another to come and follow him. After some months, he carefully selected twelve of these, to be his special companions, and in the coming time his messengers and representatives. At the time of this choice he addressed to them and the multitude the wonderful discourse called the Sermon on the Mount, which was peculiarly fitted to open up before them the true nature of the Messianic reign, and the relation of his teachings to the law of Moses and its current interpretations. For a long time the Twelve followed him about, hearing all his instructions to public assemblies or in the homes they visited, and encouraged to question him freely in private. At length he sent them out on a temporary mission in Galilee, to practise their appointed task of religious instruction. After their return he spent six months almost wholly in seclusion, in districts outside of Galilee, evidently devoting his time mainly to careful instruction of the Twelve, and at length beginning to tell them in confidence how differently his ministry would end from their expectations concerning the Messiah. Observe that although much of his teaching was private, and some things concerning the foreseen end of his ministry were to be temporarily kept to themselves, there was yet nothing here of that esoteric teaching which some ancient philosophers practised, directing that certain truths should be kept always confined to an inner circle. Jesus expressly told his disciples that what they heard in the ear they were ultimately to proclaim upon the housetops, and carry to all the nations.

The Great Teacher showed in a high degree that *patience* upon which all good teaching makes large demands. Yet we know of one occasion on which he was much displeased with the Twelve. He had been giving instruction on the important subject of divorce, and in the house the disciples were questioning him further. Just then some mothers brought to him little children for his blessing, as they were wont to do with a revered rabbi. The disciples were unwilling that this should interrupt the instructions they were seeking on so important a practical question, and so they rebuked the mothers. "But when Jesus saw it, he was moved with indignation," at their repulsing those in whom he felt so deep an interest, and from whom, as examples of docility and loving trustfulness, they themselves had so much to learn. We have seen that the reverence of his friends did not prevent familiarity, and we must add that their familiarity did not diminish reverence. As the end drew on, though it was an end which involved apparent failure and multiplied ignominy, both friend and foe manifest an awe that ever grows upon them, and cannot be shaken off.*

We may next notice that Jesus treated the *public authorities* with deference and due subjection. He said to Peter that there were reasons why he might have claimed exemption from paying the

Compare Bushnell, "Nature and the Supernatural."

annual half-shekel for the support of the temple ; and yet directed him to pay for them both. He told the disciples and the multitudes to do what the scribes bade them, because they sat on Moses' seat, were recognized interpreters of the law, but not to imitate their conduct. By a skilful and promising plot, representatives of the Pharisees and of the Herodians, or supporters of the Herod dynasty, approached him together one day, with honeyed words of flattery, asking, "Is it lawful to give tribute unto Cæsar or not?" They wished an answer, yes or no, and thought they were presenting a perfect dilemma. If he had said yes, the *Pharisees* would have gone out among the *Jews*, many of whom were very reluctant to recognize the Roman rule, and especially to pay the Roman tribute, and would have diligently used against him the offensive statement that it was proper to pay tribute to Cæsar. If he had said no, the *Herodians* would have gone to the *Roman* authorities, and charged him with encouraging the people to refuse payment of tribute, a point on which the Romans were very sensitive. It really seemed a hopeless dilemma. But he cut through the midst of it by pointing out a distinction between civil and religious duties, of which they had never thought, and which to our modern world, after being long obscured, has again become clear and cardinal, "to Cæsar the things that are Cæsar's, to God the things that are God's."

He was indeed teaching ideas that would ultimately transform society; yet he was no violent and **revolutionary** reformer, but quietly respected the existing authorities. At Gethsemane, he did not simply yield to force, he *surrendered* to representatives of the high priest, accompanied by Roman soldiers. Jesus never plunged into politics, but directly concerned himself with spiritual ideas and influences. By this course he has actually done more for civilization than could possibly have resulted had he fallen in with the common Jewish expectation and become a civil ruler. The indirect influence of his unworldly and spiritual reign is helpful to all the highest interests of humanity. Still, he could not fail to be deeply moved by the civil and social, as well as the religious condition of the chosen people. And when he wept over the foreseen destruction of Jerusalem, it was doubtless the grief of a patriot as well as of a Saviour.

In considering the association of Jesus with *the people at large,* we are struck at once with the fact that though pure and sinless, he did not shrink from contact with the most sinful and the most despised. He was in this respect the very opposite of the Pharisees. Their name signifies separatists. Fundamental in their conception of a pious life was the idea of scrupulously avoiding any social intercourse, or even the slightest contact, with persons who habitually violated the ceremonial law, as well as with those guilty of gross immorality. This was the idea of personal purity materialized, and pushed to an utter extreme. Accordingly, the Pharisees found it hard to believe that one could be a prophet, a teacher come from God, who would consent to eat at the table of a publican, or would allow his feet to be washed with the tears of a fallen woman. Jesus often found it necessary to explain and vindicate his course in this respect; and it was for this purpose that on one occasion he gave the three beautiful parables which tell of joy at the recovery of the lost sheep, the lost coin, the lost son. Contact with vile people is proper or improper according to our aim and the probable results. It must be avoided or carefully limited, if of such a character as would probably assimilate us to them. But the thoughtful and consistent followers of Jesus have been moved by his example and teachings to far more of kindly effort to redeem the vile than ever existed in the world beyond the influence of Christianity; and to do still more in this direction would only be acting according to his spirit. Jeremy Taylor has said that Jesus moved among the despised of humanity like sunshine, which falls among foul things without being itself defiled. To imitate this in our measure must be an attainment full of blessedness for us and rich in blessing to others. Jesus was very weary with months of earnest teaching as he sat that day beside Jacob's well; yet he aroused himself to speak most kindly with one who came to draw water, and that a woman who was living sinfully with a man not her husband. His conversation with her is a suggestive model of skill in the introduction of religion into private conversation—one of the finest of all accomplishments for Christian men and women. The delicate tact with which he aroused her conscience, and thus turned her thoughts away from the mere satisfaction of bodily thirst to the water of eternal life, is among the most wonderful touches in his consummate teaching.

Jesus was not only *friendly* to the poor, but he evidently counted largely, from beginning to end, on their reception of his influence and their support of his movement. He has been called "the poor man's philosopher; the first and only one that had ever appeared." * He expected, and found, the chief results of his ministry among the poor, the masses of mankind. Even ignorance may not be so great a hindrance to the sympathetic reception of moral and spiritual truth as a sophisticated culture, and a selfish contentment with existing social and moral conditions. No religious movement can have large and blessed results which does not adapt itself to the poor. No Christians are worthy to bear the name of their Master, who do not, like him, delight in preaching the gospel to the poor, and in ministering to their needs. Yet Jesus was no partisan of the poor. He also mingled freely with the rich, entering with equal freedom and equal sympathy, as his ministers should strive to do, into the lowliest and the loftiest homes.

We ought to notice how he dealt with *hypocrites*, and with the *fanatical* multitudes. Again and again he withdrew from the fanatical excitement of great crowds who thought themselves his followers, so as to leave time for such feelings to subside. Sober men of the world are at times specially disgusted with certain fanatics they hear of, and tempted to regard all apparently earnest piety as mere fanati-

* Bushnell.

cism. They ought to observe how carefully the Founder of Christianity *repressed* everything of the kind. The worst hypocrites were among men of high station or influence. These hypocrites Jesus rebuked many times, and in burning words of righteous indignation. Some have thought these words out of harmony with his characteristic gentleness and love. But it is *right* to abhor and hate all forms of vile wickedness, however we may pity the humanity that lies behind them. Many of his contemporaries imagined that the prophet of Nazareth must be one of the grand old prophets come to life again. And it is noteworthy, as a recent writer remarks,* that some thought he was Jeremiah, the tender and pathetic, while others thought he was Elijah, bold and stern in rebuking. May we not suppose that these had only observed different manifestations of a many-sided character? Or rather, that like God his Father, the compassionate love of Jesus towards human weakness was but another aspect of the same essential character which showed itself in burning indignation towards human wickedness?

Having thus gone over the principal relations which Jesus sustained in his private and public life, noticing how in each of these his character was manifested, we may now come nearer to certain *personal traits* that appear throughout the history.

The *humility* of Jesus stood in striking contrast to rabbinical and Pharisaic pride. Men often greatly wondered at his words and actions, his

* Stalker.

wisdom and power; they compared him to the most celebrated prophets, they expected him to become a more splendid king than David or Solomon; but he was gentle and humble. Moreover, he himself made the most extraordinary claims. " When the Son of man shall come in his glory, and all the angels with him, then shall he sit on the throne of his glory; and before him shall be gathered all the nations." " He that hath seen me hath seen the Father." " No one knoweth the Father, save the Son, and he to whomsoever the Son willeth to reveal him." Yet in immediate connection with this great claim he said, " Take my yoke upon you, and learn from me ; for I am meek and lowly in heart." It was indeed Jesus who caused humility to be classed among the virtues. The Greek word thus translated had in Greek literature almost always a bad sense, at best sometimes denoting modesty, the absence of arrogance ; the Latin word which we borrow made no approach to a good sense; Christianity gives to humility a notable position among virtues and graces. Yet, as if to correct the natural tendency to misapprehension in regard to this virtue, the Saviour was always eminently self-respecting, and spoke and acted with a personal dignity which even his enemies could not but recognize. When questioned by Annas, the ex-high priest, about his teaching, Jesus answered him, " I have spoken openly to the world; I ever taught in synagogues, and in the temple, where all the Jews come together ; and in secret spake I nothing. Why askest thou me ? Ask them that have heard me, what I spake unto them." To this dignified answer corresponds his dignified silence when brought before the Sanhedrin. He knew that his condemnation was a foregone conclusion. He had resolved to go straight forward to the crucifixion which awaited him. He would not condescend to answer, save when it became proper to make the decisive avowal of Messiahship. Before Pilate, who was himself a prisoner to his own previous acts of wrong-doing, and had no courage to decide according to his own sense of right, Jesus speaks with dignified compassion and quiet superiority. However hard most of us may find it to combine humility with personal dignity, yet in the Christian theory and in the Christian Exemplar they blend in perfect harmony.

The readiness of Jesus to *forgive* was often manifested. Remember his lamentation over Jerusalem: "How often would I have gathered thy children together, but ye would not." Remember how he warned Peter that headstrong self-reliance would lead him that very night into shameful and repeated denial of his Master, and yet how soon afterwards he appeared separately to the fallen but repentant disciple, forgiving and encouraging him. For the Roman soldiers who were fastening him to the cross with cruel pangs, he prayed, "Father, forgive them; for they know not what they do." Yet observe in these very words the intimation that if they *had* known what they were doing, he might not have asked that they should be forgiven. So he said in substance to Pilate, "The high priest's sin is greater than thine." Here then is no weak forgiveness of everybody for everything, penitent or impenitent, such as some people imagine to be set forth in the teachings and the example of the Founder of Christianity.

It is evident that his nature was exceedingly *sensitive.* On one occasion, when the Pharisees showed their hostility and determination not to be convinced, we are told that " he sighed deeply in his spirit." When predicting some months in advance his dread baptism of suffering he added, "and how am I straitened till it be accomplished." Once when apparently quite out of heart with the unbelief of his disciples and the multitude, he said, " O faithless generation, how long shall I be with you ? how long shall I bear with you ?" A few days before the crucifixion, after predicting his speedy death, he broke out, " Now is my soul troubled; and what shall I say ? Father, save me from this hour ? but for this cause came I unto this hour. Father, glorify thy name." No one who ever read or heard the sacred story can forget how in Gethsemane three times over he said, " If it be possible "; how on the cross he cried with a loud voice, " Why hast thou forsaken me ?" Certainly these are impressive proofs that his nature was exquisitely sensitive. And yet how patient he was! True patience is a very different thing from insensibility. Only one who feels sensitively *can* be nobly patient. In general Jesus showed great calmness. And an occasional utterance of grief and pain only sets that habitual calmness in a clearer light. The world has dwelt not too much but too exclusively on the gentle and patient traits of the Saviour's character ; and we do well to re-

mind ourselves that he also exhibited the keenest
sensibility, along with the loftiest moral courage,
the noblest strength of character.　An English
writer * has produced a little volume entitled " The
Manliness of Christ " ; and though the term may
strike us as inadequate, if not incongruous, yet it
helps to impress an important element in the Saviour's character ; for people are ever inclined to fall
back upon the notion that goodness, innocence, patience, purity belong to feeble characters, when the
fact is far otherwise.

> " How beauteous were the marks divine,
>   That in thy meekness used to shine,
>   That lit thy lonely pathway, trod
>   In wondrous love, O Son of God!
>
> " Oh, who like thee, so calm, so bright,
>   So pure, so made to live in light?
>   Oh, who like thee did ever go
>   So patient through a world of woe
>
> " Oh, who like thee so meekly bore
>   The scorn, the scoffs of men, before?
>   So meek, forgiving, godlike, high,
>   So glorious in humility?
>
> " Even death, which sets the prisoner free,
>   Was pang, and scoff, and scorn to thee ;
>   Yet love through all thy torture glowed,
>   And mercy with thy life-blood flowed.
>
> " Oh, in thy light be mine to go,
>   Illuming all my way of woe!
>   And give me ever on the road
>   To trace thy footsteps, Son of God.

With all its difficulties and sorrows, Jesus *de-
lighted in his work.*　He loved to do good, even

* Thomas Hughes.

when it appeared to be on the smallest scale. The disciples had left him worn and weary beside Jacob's well, and on their return found him alert, with beaming eyes and cheerful voice. They wondered whether any one had brought him food in their absence, and at first knew not the meaning when he said, "I have food to eat that ye know not of. My food is to do the will of him that sent me, and to accomplish his work." He had found an opportunity to do good, and the suggestion of other possibilities in those whom this poor woman might influence. Again and again we see him shaking off weariness, arousing himself with interest and delight, when there was any opening for usefulness. In the highest degree he possessed and exhibited what has been called * " an enthusiasm of humanity." He loved men, and was glad to do them good. He loved God, and it was a joy to do him honor.

At various turning-points of his ministry, we find the Saviour exercising a remarkable *prudence.* He knows what will be the consequences of a collision with the Jewish authorities, and wishes to delay the crisis until there has been time to develop his teachings and present them in every quarter of the Holy Land, and to train his chosen disciples. Accordingly, during his early ministry in Judea, when he knew that the Pharisees had heard that he was now making more disciples than his forerunner, he at once left Judea and retired to Galilee. Towards the latter part of the ministry in Galilee

* Seeley, "Ecce Homo."

he kept withdrawing into surrounding districts, to
avoid further exciting the alarm of Herod the te-
trarch, and further kindling the fanaticism of the
common people, who were bent on making him
king, and might by their excited talk have drawn
upon him the jealousy of the Roman rulers. Again
and again, at Nazareth and at Jerusalem, when
some angry crowd were about to inflict upon him mob
violence, he quietly went away. When the high
· priest and the Sanhedrin heard what had happened
to Lazarus in Bethany, and deliberately plotted the
death of Jesus, he left Jerusalem and returned no
more till the final passover. And when his "hour
was come," the quiet boldness with which he
moved forward was but the same moral courage
which he had repeatedly shown in prudently withdrawing. However men may stigmatize or ridicule prudence, it often requires and manifests the
highest courage. Remember too that his prudence
was united with transparent sincerity. We can
clearly see combined in him, what he bade his disciples cultivate, the prudence of the serpent and the
simplicity of the dove.

And now the most remarkable thing about this
strong, sensitive, richly developed, beautifully symmetrical character, the wonderful thing which can
be said of him alone among all the good and noble
of human history is this: his character stands out
as faultless, perfect. So thoroughly symmetrical is
this character in all its proportions that the
careless observer does not realize to what an
extent it is at the same time great and strong.
Yet as it grows to our thoughtful contemplation,

grows exalted and sublime, it is so harmonious as still to appear simple and winning. Can it indeed be that in this world of ours, in this our human nature, there has been a character really and absolutely perfect ? Men who do not believe in the Saviour's divine mission and personal claims have been naturally slow to admit that he was perfect; and some of them have keenly searched among all the abounding details of his action and speech for some ground of fault-finding. All that I know of as said in this direction at the present day would be the following points. Theodore Parker * suggested that his driving out the money-changers from the temple, with uplifted scourge, shows unseemly anger and violence. But to ordinary sober judgment it is plain that the anger was seemly enough and richly deserved; while the uplifted scourge was but a symbol of authority and reminder of ill-desert, like many an object-lesson taught by the old prophets. Some have complained that he pronounced a curse upon a fig-tree which by its leaves made pretence of having also fruit. But this withered fig-tree has stood as another object-lesson to all the ages, full of instruction; and there is not the slightest indication or reason to suppose that the curse was pronounced from any wrong personal feeling. Francis William Newman, skeptical brother of the great cardinal, censured the Saviour for quietly yielding himself to death when he could so easily have avoided it. But this reproach was accepted beforehand, for Jesus declared that like a

---

* Bushnell.

good shepherd, he *voluntarily* laid down his life for
the sheep. A well-known American lecturer
against the Bible once almost found fault with Jesus for something or other, but I really do not even
remember what it was. It seems idle to discuss, and
almost useless to mention, such points as these ; but
the fact that perverse ingenuity can indicate no
semblance of fault in Jesus that will bear the sim-
plest inquiry, only brings us back to the conclusion
already reached, that he stands out before us as
really faultless and perfect. During his ministry,
the Jewish rulers repeatedly charged him with de-
ceiving the people, but at the trial before the Sanhedrin, they could adduce nothing but silly and
contradictory perversions of what he had said, and
they finally condemned him only upon his own avowal
that he was the Messiah, which the high priest declared to be in itself an act of blasphemy. Before all
history, Jesus of Nazareth stands as sinless, even
as he himself one day said in the temple court,
" Which of you convicteth me of sin ? " It might
indeed be suggested that the evangelists have only
carried unusually far the tendency of biographers
to keep faults in the background. But read, and
you see that they freely record varied accusations
made against him, and often without stopping to
reply; while they relate his profoundest sayings
and most astonishing actions with such simplicity
and quietness of tone as to constitute a unique literary phenomenon.

Yet this perfect character stands before us as inviting imitation. Its outward conditions do not
withdraw him from our sympathy and make imita-

tion seem difficult, for he did not live as a king, or as a retired student, or a recluse ascetic. His example is not like a copy set with intricate flourishes, but in clear and simple lines, perfectly beautiful, but not discouraging the effort to imitate.* Of him alone among all ethical teachers can it be said that to imitate his example and to obey his precepts would amount to precisely the same thing. It is a remarkable statement which John Stuart Mill, trained from childhood to disbelief of the Bible, makes in one of his posthumous " Essays on Religion," that it would not even now " be easy, even for an unbeliever, to find a better translation of the rule of virtue from the abstract into the concrete, than to endeavor so to live that Christ would approve our life."

The German scholar Rothe is quoted as saying in his work on Ethics, " I know no other ground on which I could anchor my whole being, and particularly my speculations, except that historical phenomenon, Jesus Christ. He is to me the unimpeachable Holy of Holies of humanity, ... and a sun-rising in history whence has come the light by which we see the world."

How strongly attractive, to all who will dwell upon it thoughtfully, is the personality of Jesus the Saviour. All around us are children who as they study the Sunday School lessons from the gospels, feel their tender hearts drawn out to love Jesus, to confide in him, to follow him though unseen. And for us all, however mature and instructed, it would

*Isaac Barrow.

assuredly be the best fruit of the historical spirit, the summit of true philosophy, the crown of all culture, to read afresh these gospel records with the simplicity of a little child, and learn to love and confide in Jesus.

II.

The Ethical Teachings of Jesus.

THE ETHICAL TEACHINGS OF JESUS.

IT is a notable characteristic of Christianity that the ethical teachings of its Founder are insepa-rably connected with his religious teachings. "Thou shalt love thy neighbor as thyself" is not given by him as a separate and detached precept, but as one of two. "Thou shalt love the Lord thy God with all thy heart, and with all thy soul, and with all thy mind. This is the great and first commandment. And a second like unto it is this, thou shalt love thy neighbor as thyself. On these two command-ments hangeth the whole law and the prophets." Observe that the two precepts are not simply placed side by side, they are united: "on these two." In like manner the first four of the ten commandments present duties to God, the others present duties to men; the opening petitions of the Lord's Prayer are that God may be honored, the others that we may be blessed. In the great judgment scene de-scribed by Jesus, where he himself will sit as king, the rewards and punishments of the future life are made to turn upon the performance or the neglect of duties to him in the person of his people. Every-thing religious in Christianity is made to furnish a motive to morality.

We all condemn the fanatics who would make religion sufficient without ethics. Some teachings of this sort are absurd, and some disgusting. But on the other hand, shall we think it wise to regard ethics as sufficient without religion? Is it not true that he who would divorce religion and morality is an enemy to religion, and at best only a mistaken friend to morality?

Among the Greeks and Romans, in the historical period, these two were little connected. They were not even generally taught by the same persons; the priests taught religion, the philosophers taught morality. Some of the actions ascribed to the deities themselves were grossly immoral. The Jewish contemporaries of Jesus were severely rebuked by him for their traditional directions as to Corban. A man might refuse food to his own father by saying that this particular food was Corban, a thing offered to God, thus setting aside for the sake of a supposed religious service the profound moral obligation and the express commandment of God's law, to honor father and mother. So likewise Jesus pronounced woes upon the hypocritical Pharisees for scrupulously tithing the least important vegetables that grew in their gardens, and then leaving " undone the weightier matters of the law, justice and mercy and faith "; for carefully cleansing the outside of the cup and the dish, while their contents were the product of extortion and excess.

Ethical obligation, according to the Saviour's teachings, is enforced by the yet higher religious obligation. Our duties to men are really a part of our all-comprehensive duty to God. *Why* must I love my neighbor as myself? If it be placed on utilitarian grounds, meaning personal utility, then I ought to love my neighbor as myself because it will benefit me, that is, because I love myself better than my neighbor. If the utility consulted be general, then *why* ought I to care as much for the general good as for my own? We are back where we started. Herbert Spencer, with all the ability and earnestness shown in his " Data of Ethics," makes a reply which I think men in general cannot recognize as philosophically conclusive or practically cogent. Natural sympathy with others, we are told, if frequently exercised, hardens by force of habit into altruism, a sense of obligation to others. Is that all? Nay, I must love my neighbor as myself because I am the creature and the child of God, whom I must love with all my heart, more than my neighbor and more than myself. Shall we then, it may be asked, accuse every man who is not definitely religious of being gravely immoral? Nay, individual moral convictions may be largely the result of inheritance, education and present environment, and may subsist notwithstanding the individual lack of those religious convictions which are their proper, and, as a general fact, their actual support.

Observe further that Jesus not only tells us what we ought to do, but shows how we may be able to do so. He presents in his own character and life an inspiring example, satisfying our noblest ideal of morality, and yet conforming itself to the conditions of our own existence. He tells how we may obtain divine assistance in obeying his precepts.

Many other teachers have given wholesome precepts, but left men to keep them in their unaided
strength. Jesus tells of a divinely-wrought change
so thorough as to be called a new birth, of a divine
spiritual help which our heavenly Father will
readily give. It is in this, and not simply in the
great superiority of his precepts, that we find the
unapproachable excellence of the Christian ethics.

In connection with this point we must remember
that Jesus constantly pre-supposes the sinfulness of
human nature. Many ethical precepts, and even
whole systems of ethics, appear to assume that men
have no particular bias toward evil. But it is far
otherwise with him ; and he meets the demands of
the situation by providing atonement, renewal and
divine sanctification.

Another thing quite without parallel is the
unique authority which these ethical instructions
derive from the faultless life and character of the
Teacher himself. Every other instructor in morals
comes manifestly short of his own standard, as indeed befalls the teacher in every other department
of practical human exertion. Even the lessons
given by the best parents to their children are subject to inevitable discount on account of the faults
in parental character and conduct of which the
children are aware and the parents are conscious.
Here alone among all moral instructors the example
is absolutely equal to the precept.

Are the ethical teachings of Jesus *original ?*
Some have thought this a question of great importance. Opponents have taken immense pains to
show that certain of his precepts find a partial

parallel in previously existing pagan writings ; and some Christian apologists have been nervously unwilling to recognize the fact. It needs no great reflection to see that a wise teacher of morals must bring his instructions into close connection with what men already know, or what they will instinctively recognize as true when suggested by his lessons. If you are teaching a child, you do not present ideas entirely apart from and above the child's previous consciousness ; you try to link the new thoughts to what the child has thought of before. We need not then be at all unwilling to admit that for the most part Jesus only carried farther and lifted higher and extended more widely the views of ethical truth which had been dimly caught by the universal human mind, or had at least been seen by the loftiest souls. This was but a part of the wisdom of his teachings. The most familiar and striking instance is the so-called golden rule, something more or less similar to which is ascribed to various contemporaries of Jesus and to earlier teachers. Thus Hillel said, " What is hateful to thee, do not do to another," and he was but repeating a passage in the book of Tobit, " What thou hatest, do to no one." A Greek biographer of Aristotle relates that being asked how we should behave towards our friends he answered, " As we should wish them to behave towards us "; and Isocrates had previously said, " What you are angry at when inflicted on you by others, this do not do to others." A similar negative form of the precept is also frequently quoted from Confucius, " What you do not like when done

to yourself, do not do to others." But Confucius
really taught, though not in form, the positive side
of the same idea. A follower asked, " Is there one
word which may serve as a rule of practice for all
one's life ? " Confucius replied, " Is not reciprocity such a word ? What you do not want done to
yourself, do not do to others." Dr. R. H. Graves,
a distinguished missionary for many years in Can-
ton, who went from Baltimore, replies to my inquiries that " reciprocity " seems to be a fairly
correct translation. And this saying of the Ana-
lects is in the doctrine of the mean so illustrated as
to leave no doubt that Confucius intended a positive, and not merely a negative precept. I have
taken pains to bring out this fact as a matter of simple justice and exact truth. And indeed if we did
not gladly " seize upon truth where'er 'tis found,"
we should not be faithful to the spirit of Jesus.

A recent writer * has pointed out that the Christian ethical system harmoniously *combines* principles which had been separately emphasized by the
Greek philosophers. The Epicurean laid stress on
self-love; the Stoic on love for others; the Platonist
on love to God, in a certain limited sense. There
can indeed be no basis for moral conduct other than
" the love of self, the love of humanity, the love of
God; and the religion which unites these has become
the foundation of absolute morality." This is not at
all saying that Jesus *derived* these ideas from the
pagan philosophers. In fact they reside in the
moral nature of man, and his relations to the nature

* Matheson, " Landmarks of New Testament Morality."

of things and to the Creator. Jesus combines in harmonious completeness truths which one or another had separately and imperfectly taught.

The Old Testament ethical teachings he assumes as already received among his hearers, and in a general way endorses. The two foundation precepts, as to love of God and love of our neighbor, were both drawn from the law of Moses, though not there given together, nor either of them presented as fundamental. But have we not been frequently told of late that Jesus undertook to revolutionize the Old Testament ethics? Did he not supplant the law of Moses by his own authoritative and better teachings? No, nothing of the kind. He expressly declared in the Sermon on the Mount, that he came not to destroy the law, as some Jews imagined the Messiah would do in order to make life easier, but came to *complete* the law. And the examples which follow this statement are not at all examples of teaching contrary to the law of Moses, but in every case of going *further in the same direction.* Thus the law condemned killing; he condemns hate and anger. The law forbade adultery; he declared that a lustful look is virtual adultery. The law forbade false swearing; he goes further and commands not to swear at all. The only saying he condemns is the phrase, "and hate thine enemy"; but this was not a part of the law, it was a Rabbinical addition, " Thou shalt love thy neighbor, and hate thine enemy." And the only case in which he appears to condemn an ethical teaching actually found in the Old Testament is really to the same effect as the others. The Mosaic

law of divorce was really a restriction upon the
otherwise existing facility of divorce, in that the
preparation of a document gave time for reflection,
and the possession of it afforded some protection to
the wife turned away.   Jesus was going further in
the same direction when he restricted divorce within
narrower limits.   And while he said that Moses for
the hardness of their hearts allowed divorce for
various causes, his own teaching expressly went
back to the original constitution of human beings as
laid down in the Old Testament.   There is thus no
ground for the assertion that Jesus taught as a
revolutionary reformer, or proposed to set aside the
Old Testament ethics as essentially erroneous.   He
always went further in the same direction, he com-
pleted the law.

It is often asserted by some modern writers that
the Founder of Christianity derived much of his
teaching from the current traditions of Rabbinical
sayings, as shown by the existence of similar ideas
or expressions in the Talmud and other late Jewish
writings.   The alleged proofs of this indebtedness
are few and curiously inadequate.   It is folly to
say that Jesus derived the golden rule from his
older contemporary, Hillel, for we have seen that it
existed centuries before.   The statement is frequently made that the Lord's Prayer is all found in
the Talmud or in the liturgies now used in synagogues.   I have investigated all the proofs of this
adduced by accessible writers, and the facts are as
follows: the only exact parallels presented in the
Talmud and the liturgies are to the address, " Our
Father, who art in heaven," and the two petitions,

" Hallowed be thy name," and " Bring us not into temptation." There are phrases somewhat resembling " Thy kingdom come," and " Deliver us from the evil one." There is no parallel to " Thy will be done, as in heaven, so on earth," or to " Give us this day our daily bread," or to the petition which Jesus emphasized by repeating it after the prayer, " Forgive us our debts, as we also have forgiven our debtors." Thus the most characteristic petitions of the prayer are wholly without Jewish parallel, and the scattered phrases similar to some of its expressions are such as devout Jews could hardly fail sometimes to employ. The image of the mote and the beam, and two or three other expressions elsewhere employed by Jesus, are found in the Talmud. They may have been proverbial. Or it is entirely possible that the Talmud and other late Jewish writings really borrowed sometimes from the New Testament. The Jews in Alexandria early borrowed largely from the Greek philosophers, and at a later period the Jews are said to have borrowed from the Arabs; why might they not adopt an occasional phrase from the Christian writers, whom they could so easily claim as really of their own race? Thus the charge of indebtedness to Hillel, or to the traditions in general, so far as I can find evidence, quite breaks down.*

Let us next consider that the ethical teachings of Jesus do not usually undertake to give mere rules, but to set forth principles. The Jewish traditions had run everything into rules. They called it

* Comp. Delitzsch, "Jesus and Hillel."

making a fence around the law, to encompass it
with all manner of minute directions, which would
keep men away from breaking the law. It is a
general tendency of mankind to save themselves the
trouble of thinking, by expressing principles in the
form of rules. Many schools and some colleges
undertake to regulate the whole behavior of the
student by a set of rules; and churches sometimes
show the same tendency. Jesus evidently set himself against this disposition. He did not wish his
followers to be burdened by stiff and narrow rules;
he taught them principles, which are at once more
comprehensive and more flexible. And the thinking which is required in order to apply principles brings with it a most valuable part of our
moral discipline.

Some sayings of Jesus have often been taken for
rules which were meant only as striking statements
of a principle; for example, "Whosoever smiteth
thee on thy right cheek, turn to him the other also."
If any proof be needed that this was not meant as a
rule, let us judge of the Saviour's meaning from the
course which he himself pursued, for he, as we have
said before, is the one teacher whose example never
fell short of his precepts. When one of the high
priest's officers struck him at the trial, we do not
read that he turned the other cheek. He calmly
remonstrated: "If I have spoken evil, bear witness
of the evil; but if well, why smitest thou me?"
Here, as in many other cases, we can interpret his
saying by his action. In like manner he said,
"Resist not him that is evil;" and many have taken
this as a rule and have inferred that war is always

wrong, and that a man must never defend himself when attacked. Yet Jesus did not tell the believing centurion at Capernaum to abandon his calling, nor in any case intimate that it was wrong to be a soldier. We must remember that the Saviour was often a field-preacher, or a preacher in public squares. It was necessary to hold the attention of his audience, whom no decorum restrained from leaving. Some had never heard him before, some would never hear him again; it was necessary to drive a truth into unsympathetic minds, to fix it there in permanent remembrance. He did this partly by a great variety of images and illustrations, and partly by paradoxical statements which would compel reflection and ensure recollection. Thus the saying, "Turn to him the other cheek also," has been very often misunderstood, and may have been misunderstood by some of those who first heard it; but did any one ever forget that saying? Better that many should misunderstand, than that none should remember. We interpret such sayings by their general connection, or by the Saviour's own example, or his teaching on other occasions. This is a very different thing from explaining away his teachings because not in accordance with our views or wishes; this is only trying to determine what he really meant. He said, "Swear not at all," and many persons, including some devoted Christians, have understood that he forbids taking an oath in a court of justice. Yet they ought to have noticed that he himself did that very thing. The high priest presiding in the Sanhedrin said, "I put thee on oath by the living God, that thou tell us whether

thou art the Christ, the Son of God." To answer
at all was to answer on oath; and Jesus answered.
So then his prohibition of swearing must have re-
lated to the sadly common use of oaths in ordinary
conversation. His example interprets his precept.

Again he said, " Give to him that asketh thee."
People suppose that here is a rule for unrestricted
observance, though perhaps no one in real life ever
attempted to carry it out. But in the same discourse
he said, "Ask, and it shall be given you." In this
latter case he goes on to compare the heavenly
Father's giving to that of parents. These, with all
their human infirmity, "know how" to give good
things to their children, and will not weakly give
what the children ask through mistake; much more
must the Father in heaven know how to give, and
withhold where that would be truer kindness. Then
if the promise as to God's giving what we ask is limited by the nature of the case, so must be the direction to give to others what they ask of us. He also
says, " Love your enemies. . . . that ye may be
sons of your Father who is in heaven." Yet the
heavenly Father does not love enemies *as* he loves
friends; he cannot love enemies with a love of com-
placency, as he loves the obedient and holy. " He
maketh his sun to rise on the evil and the good,
and sendeth rain on the just and the unjust." So
we should love our enemies, and gladly do them
good; but this does not mean that we ought to love
them as we love our friends.

In like manner then we must interpret what the
Saviour said as to revenge. The law of Moses
confined the requital of injuries to exact retaliation,

" an eye for an eye, and a tooth for a tooth," while natural human passion would tend to make the requital far surpass the injury. Jesus goes further in the same direction as the law, and entirely forbids revenge. So great an evil is revenge, so carefully must we avoid it, that he says, better give the litigant the exempted garment as well as the other, better invite still further exactions from the impressing officer, better turn the other cheek for a second blow, than to practise revenge. I repeat, we must not explain away the Saviour's sayings to suit our own notions, but we must seek to ascertain his real meaning. And I think it is clear that some of these sayings were not at all designed to be taken as rules, but were only a paradoxical or otherwise striking expression of a principle.

Because of these paradoxical expressions many have declared the morality taught by Jesus to be unpractical, and so have disregarded any and all of his teachings as much as they please. Some sincerely devout persons have excused themselves for falling short of other precepts on the ground that several of his sayings could not be literally obeyed. Some Christians have made a point of refusing to bear arms, or to practise any sort of resistance to wrong. Count Tolstoi, a man of great imagination and dramatic power, but morbid and a trifle fantastical, supposes himself to have discovered, as a new thing in the world, that Jesus meant these paradoxical statements of a principle for precise rules. He does not know that the same notion has been held by some persons in almost every age and country. And the gifted old nobleman tries to live

according to his discovery, so far as his own wiser
instincts and the control of those around him will
allow. Tell him that if such notions were generally
adopted it would break up society, and like many
others of his countrymen at the present day, he
would reply that society ought to be completely
demolished, so that we may see if the survivors
cannot build something better. In like manner
Ibsen in one of his dramas makes the hero attempt
to act upon these sayings as rules, but shows that
the result must be to crush the individual attempt-
ing it, and supposes himself thereby to prove that
the existing constitution of society in Christian
countries is wholly contrary to the real teachings of
the Founder of Christianity. But did Jesus ever
mean thus to teach? Has he not been simply
misunderstood?

We turn now to consider the great *motive* which
Jesus connects with his ethical teachings. That
motive, as already intimated, and as well known, is
Love. The love of God is to be supreme. The
love of one's neighbor is to be in equipoise with the
love of self. This makes a distinct recognition of
self-love as essentially right. And Jesus elsewhere
appeals to self-interest in the highest sense, saying,
" It is profitable for thee," " What shall it profit a
man?" Nor was this self-love forbidden by the self-
renunciation which he enjoined. One who proposed
to be his follower must renounce himself, and take
up his cross, and follow on as ready to be crucified.
And so it is added, " Whosoever shall lose his life
for my sake shall find it." Self-renunciation for his
sake was thus encouraged by a higher self-love.

In sinful beings self-love constantly gravitates downwards towards selfishness. The remedy is to keep it balanced by love of our neighbor, while love to God is exalted above both, and holds them in symmetrical relation. A man's duties to himself, as accordant with and implied in Christ's teachings, would form a wholesome subject of reflection and discussion. An English literary man tells us, "The philosophy of the past said, Know thyself; the philosophy of the present says, Improve thyself." In sooth, neither of these will make much progress without the other.

Yet the powerful instinct of self-love needs far less encouragement in ethico-religious teaching than the disposition to love our neighbor. Accordingly, the one is simply implied in the teachings of Jesus, the other is repeatedly and strongly urged. The race antagonisms and national animosities which so abounded in the world that Christianity entered, which caused every foreigner to be instinctively regarded as an enemy, led the Jewish Rabbinical instructors to quibble with the command, "Thou shalt love thy neighbor as thyself." They would say, Certainly, but who *is* my neighbor? A dog of a Gentile is not my neighbor. An abominable Samaritan is not my neighbor. And so there arose the fashion of making an addition to the law, " Thou shalt love thy neighbor, and hate thine enemy." It is easy to exclaim against the scribes and lawyers for such a gloss; but it ought to be a warning. We are all in danger of adding to, or subtracting from, or somehow modifying, a law of man or a law of God that interferes with our interests, passions or prejudices. We read that a certain lawyer, that is a professional student of the law of Moses, undertook one day to test the wisdom of Jesus by asking, " Teacher, what shall I do to inherit eternal life ? And he said unto him, What is written in the law ? How readest thou ? And he answering said, Thou shalt love the Lord thy God with all thy heart, and with all thy soul, and with all thy mind; and thy neighbor as thyself." Here we see that at least some of the Jewish teachers were already accustomed to put the two commandments together. And Jesus said unto him, " Thou hast answered right; this do, and thou shalt live. But he, desiring to justify himself, said unto Jesus, And who is my neighbor ? " This shows the process above mentioned. He wished to justify himself for a conscious lack of general benevolence by restricting the definition of the term neighbor. Having perceived this, we see the point of the Saviour's reply in the parable of the Good Samaritan. A Jew fell among robbers, who left him half dead. Two of his own people, not merely private citizens, but one a priest and the other a Levite, successively saw his hapless plight and kept on the other side of the way. Presently he was relieved, with kindliest care, by a Samaritan. Let us be thankful that with all our modern bad feeling of many kinds, we find it hard to realize the burning hatred which existed between the Jews and the Samaritans: a hatred compounded of race antagonism, oft-repeated national strife, utter non-intercourse socially or even in business, and religious bigotry and jealousy. The point is then that a neighbor, in the sense of the law, is even one of the most hostile and hated, scorned and loathed, of human beings, when you find him needing human help. Notice in this case, as heretofore, how strongly the Great Teacher presents a general truth by a single illustrative example. If Jew and Samaritan were to be neighbors, in the sense of the law, there could be no limit within the bounds of universal humanity. Wherever we see need, we see a neighbor. And the priest and the Levite, stepping along the opposite side of the road, are a warning to all religious officials, who have no taste, or fancy they have no time, for the relief of suffering humanity.

We must observe that in general Jesus did not merely enjoin the duty of caring for others. The whole tendency of his teachings, his example, the spirit he infuses, has always been to awaken a burning enthusiasm for the relief, the improvement, the increased welfare of our fellow-men. Make liberal concession, far more liberal than any known facts might indicate, as to the human kindness often manifested before Christ came, yet every one must acknowledge that Christianity has in this respect given a new meaning to such words as benevolence and humanity. With all the misapprehensions and corruptions of Christian teaching which have prevailed, with all the grievous imperfections and inconsistencies so widely existing among professed Christians, yet the story of Christian benevolence, in its various departments and throughout the Christian ages, shines among the fairest and most inspiring pages of human history. And how far its best specimens fall short of the original author and exemplar!

Many have considered that the Saviour's teachings as to forgiveness were impracticable; that to forgive seven times a day, to forgive till seventy times seven, to forgive those who trespass against us, or else we cannot hope that our Heavenly Father will forgive our trespasses against him, belongs to some lofty ideal that we may admire like the stars, but to which ordinary humanity can never climb up. But is there not an important distinction here between forgiveness and the love of enemies? We may illustrate again by the example of God himself. He does not forgive his enemies until they repent and change into friends; yet he loves his enemies who have not repented, and sends upon them rain and sunshine, the common blessings of his Providence. So we ought to love those who have wronged us, and be glad to do them any kindness which would not promote their evil designs against us; but we are under no obligation, in fact we have no right to forgive them in the strict sense of the term, to restore them to our confidence and affection, until they repent, until we have good reason to believe that they will henceforth act otherwise. If this be the correct idea of Christian forgiveness, it is not impracticable, and we should not exempt or excuse ourselves from performing the duty so often enjoined. As to love of enemies, with all the imperfection of our actual Christianity, it has wrought a great change in the views and feelings of mankind. Among the ancients "that man considered himself fortunate who on his death-bed could say, in reviewing his past life, that no one had done more good to his friends or more mischief to his enemies. This was the celebrated felicity of Sulla; this is the crown of Xenophon's panegyric on Cyrus the Younger." The author of " Ecce Homo" adds, " When therefore people deliberately consider it mean to forgive extreme injuries, they are really setting a limit, not to the duty of forgiveness, but to the possibility of genuine repentance. The words 'there are some injuries that no one ought to forgive,' mean really 'there are some injuries of which it is impossible to repent.'" And again, " The forgiveness of injuries, which was regarded in the ancient world as a virtue indeed, but an almost impossible one, appears to the moderns in ordinary cases a plain duty. . . And so a new virtue has been introduced into human life." Many in Christian countries still practice unforgiving hatred and even ferocious revenge, but few defend it, and all know that it is utterly forbidden by Christianity.

A kindred subject will be our Lord's teachings as to *the poor.* The Jews have always been in an eminent degree lovers of money, and gifted in acquiring it, being in that, as in most respects, one of the foremost races of mankind. They interpreted the Old Testament promises of providential reward and punishment to the effect that if a man was prosperous and rich it showed him to be an uncommonly good man, a favorite of heaven ; and if he was poor and suffering, this was the punishment of his uncommon sinfulness. So the friends of Job insisted that he must have been guilty of great sins, though nobody knew what they were, for here was the manifest penalty and proof in his great sufferings. If a Jew had passed by and observed the scene described in the parable of the rich man and Lazarus, his natural thought would have been, yonder man of wealth must be a very good man, and this poor wretch at the gate must have been very wicked. Now the author of the parable made it teach the opposite of their views in this case. He did not mean that all rich men are bad, and will one day lift up their eyes, being in torment, nor that all poor men are good, but he gave a case in point, diametrically opposed to Jewish opinion. Yet even here the dying beggar was carried by angels into the bosom of Abraham, who had been a Prince of the East, a man of great wealth. Jesus rebuked the Jewish error as to riches and poverty, showed himself the friend of the poor, and found among them the great majority of his followers. Yet the family at Bethany, whom he especially loved, were manifestly rich. One of the sisters had a box of perfumery, which was declared by a man interested in money-values, named Judas Iscariot, to be worth more than three hundred denaries. Now a denary was the common price of a day's labor, and, allowing for Sabbaths and feast-days, this box of perfumery was worth more than a whole year's work of a laboring man. Mary of Bethany could not have possessed it, or if possessing by gift or inheritance, could not have rightly used it in an unpractical way, had they not been a wealthy family—which also accounts for the fact that " many of the Jews " went out from Jerusalem to the suburban village to comfort the sisters when their brother died. The Saviour had the previous day commended the holy enthusiasm of a poor widow, who gave more than all the rich, gave all she had to live on. And here he justifies Mary for using this costly article of luxury in a quite unpractical expression of affection, though there were thousands of poor in the great city two miles away. The occasion was extraordinary, she was showing that she understood better than the Twelve the Master's intimations of his approaching death, and that the recognition of it did not weaken her faith or her love, and " she did what she could " to cheer him as the dark shadows gathered. But though the incident was extraordinary in its circumstances, it certainly proves that wealthy people may sometimes lawfully express affection to God or man by costly gifts, though there be many all around who are poor and needy.

The words of Jesus to the young ruler, " Sell all thou hast and give to the poor, and thou shalt have treasure in heaven; and come, follow me," are often spoken of as if he had enjoined this upon all who propose to follow him. Yet there is no record of his laying such requirement upon any one else, except that Matthew the publican and the two sons of Zebedee left their business to follow him as permanently attached disciples. The " one thing " lacked by the young ruler was that he should not only care much for eternal life, but care *more* for it than all things else. The test was, whether he would sacrifice what he valued most in this world, out of supreme devotion to Jesus. That which he valued most was his vast wealth, and this test he could not stand. The test for another man would be whether out of devotion to Jesus he could abandon sinful pleasures, or relinquish worldly ambitions. The principle involved is that the service of God must be supreme. In a certain sense, " religion must be everything, or it is nothing." One who retains or acquires wealth, one who pursues ambition or indulges in pleasures, must subordinate all to his Christian discipleship, or he is no disciple.

It was to Jewish hearers an almost unequalled paradox to say, " How hard is it for a rich man to enter into the kingdom of heaven. It is easier for a camel to pass through the eye of a needle." Various and strange attempts have been made to explain away this comparison. Yet it is an obvious hyperbole—the largest familiar animal passing through the smallest familiar orifice, representing impossibility. The Talmud has a similar saying, only substituting the elephant, a still larger animal. The disciples understood Jesus as meaning an impossibility, for they replied, " Who then *can* be saved ? " If the rich cannot, who can be ? And Jesus answered, " With men it is impossible ; but with God all things are possible." On the other hand, the Sermon on the Mount begins with a series of sayings quite the reverse of Jewish opinion. This opinion was, Happy the rich, the well-fed, the merry, those who taste the sweetness of revenge. Jesus says, Happy the poor, the hungry, the mourners, the meek and merciful, the peacemakers. Why should the poor be called happy ? Because they were more likely to accept the good

news of the Messianic reign, and thus to enjoy its
high spiritual blessing; because the poor in possessions were more likely to become the poor in spirit.
This reconciles for us the phrase in Luke, " Happy
are ye poor," with that in Matthew, " Happy are the
poor in spirit." In like manner the Saviour more
than once set it forth as a sign of his Messiahship, a
sign predicted by Isaiah, " To the poor the gospel is
preached." It requires an almost impossible effort
of historical imagination to appreciate the change
which Christianity has wrought in the feelings of
mankind with regard to the poor. Still, alas !
even in Christian countries, they are often despised
and neglected and wronged. But this much at
least is true, that all men know it ought to be
otherwise, and that very many strive, in various
and helpful ways, to have it otherwise. Jesus of
Nazareth has been the best friend the poor have
ever had in human history ; and his faithful and
wise followers will try in this also to be like him.
Yet we have seen that he was no enemy of wealth,
that he had special friends and devoted followers
who were wealthy; and there is nothing in his
teachings to encourage the notion that equality in
human possessions is desirable or possible.

In this connection it may be well to make a slight
digression, and notice a very common and very
grave misunderstanding as to the generosity of the
Saviour's followers in Jerusalem during the years
that immediately succeeded his departure. The
phrase is used in Acts, " they had all things common " ; and it is stated that even the holders of
real estate would sell it and bring the money to

the Apostles for the support of the brethren. Hence the idea has grown widely current that these Christians at Jerusalem were really Communists, that every one who joined them at once gave up his entire possessions to a common fund, and there was no longer any private ownership ; and from this supposed fact various inferences have been drawn by friend and foe. But it is not a fact. It can be proven from the record that they were not Communists. When Ananias sold a piece of land, and brought a part of the proceeds to the Apostles, making the impression that he had brought all, as others were doing, Peter said to him, " While it remained, did it not remain thine own ? and after it was sold, was it not in thy power ? " His sin was not in withholding a part, but in lying to inspired men, lying against God. Now this language of Peter is absolutely incompatible with the idea that every Christian at once gave up all his property to a common fund. The Apostle declares that the property was his own while it remained unsold ; and that after it was sold, the money was in his own power. He was under no necessity of selling, or of turning over the proceeds. Think of it, and this clearly shows that no real Communism prevailed among them. What then is meant by the phrase, "they had all things common " ? It means that they held all their property as for the common benefit. Listen : " and not one of them said that aught of the things which he possessed was his own ; but they had all things common." No one *said* that any part of his property was his own ; it *was* his own, but he did not so speak of it; he regarded and treated his property as held for the benefit of his brethren. A reader of the Greek will notice that here and throughout the following passage every verb is in the imperfect tense, showing what happened from time to time, as the brethren saw need and felt moved: " as many as were possessors of lands or houses sold them, and brought the prices of the things that were sold, and laid them at the Apostles' feet; and distribution was made unto each, according as any one had need." Every verb is in the imperfect tense. (Acts 4: 32-35; likewise in 2: 43-47.) One Christian this month, and another the next month, would bring money, even selling property for the purpose; and this went on during the several years embraced in the first six chapters of Acts. Thus you see that this was not at all a case of Communism. It was a case of extraordinary generosity, called for by extraordinary needs. Many of these first believers had come up to the great Pentecost, with only money enough for a short visit and a return, and here they were remaining for months and years; others had been fishermen on the Lake of Galilee, and at Jerusalem had no means of livelihood; others were poor Jews at Jerusalem, accustomed to receive help from the contributions of wealthy Jews in foreign countries, and cut off from this as soon as they became Christians. Rejoicing together in their new faith and hope and love, those of them who had property gladly contributed, as they saw occasion, for the support of their brethren. All this ceased of course when the disciples were scattered in every direction by the persecution that arose in connection with Stephen. And it is greatly to be regretted that this magnificent example of Christian generosity should be popularly mistaken for an attempt at Communism, and even sometimes represented as turning out to be impracticable, and thereby showing itself to be unwise.

The fact that in this and various other cases the ethical teachings of Christianity have been widely misunderstood, must not prevent us from recognizing and endeavoring fully to appreciate how much the Saviour really taught that was new to the world, and among the greatest blessings ever brought to mankind. When he said " give to him that asketh," it was (as we have seen) not a mere rule, requiring or authorizing us to scatter alms with blind negligence, since God, who is held forth as our example, gives to those who ask him, but gives wisely; and yet it is a precept that stirs every true Christian heart to benevolence. Whether we shall give to needy individuals upon casual application, or shall in general prefer to give through carefully organized effort, is a question of expediency and practical wisdom ; but in some way, yea, in all ways that are not palpably unwise, we must give. And it is in accordance with the whole spirit of Christianity that we should not merely relieve human suffering, but that we should strive to prevent it. The principles which Jesus taught will be found to apply with the most flexible adaptation to whatever may be required and justified by our growing knowledge of sanitary and social conditions.

I should be very glad, if we had time, to dwell
on many details of the Saviour's ethical instruction.
Especially should I like to show—what we all
know in a general way—how he has put unspeakable honor upon the lowlier and more passive virtues, which the pride of human strength is so apt
to neglect or even to despise. But it is impossible
now to attempt any detailed exhibition of his moral
teachings. I know of no one who questions that as
a whole they are greatly superior to those of any
other teacher, or of all other teachers combined.
The only drawback with some minds has been the
existence of certain sayings supposed to be impracticable, and these I have tried to show have been simply misunderstood. The only ethical teachings now
compared by any one with those of Jesus are the
ethics found in the Buddhist writings. Let us gladly recognize all in these that is true and wholesome,
and the great good they have done on a wide scale
in the Asiatic world, as supplanting ideas that
formerly prevailed among many races. The recent
fashion of favorably comparing Buddhism with
Christianity has been thought by some to find
countenance in Sir Edwin Arnold's poem, "The
Light of Asia." It may have been justifiable in a
poem that he should borrow Christian terms, and
add no small tinge of Christian sentiments, in order
to make pleasing poetry for Christian readers; the
trouble is that many have failed to distinguish in
this case between a poem and a history. As I
heartily admire many parts of "The Light of Asia,"
I am glad to quote words taken down from the author's lips during his recent voyage across the

Pacific by a man whom I personally know to be of the highest character and intelligence. Sir Edwin said to Dr. Ashmore, " I have been criticised for an implied comparison between Buddhism and Christianity in regard to doctrines derived from them and principles contained in them respectively. No such object was in mind. For me Christianity rightly viewed is the crowned queen of religions, immensely superior to every other, and though I am so great an admirer of much that is great in Hindu philosophy and religion, I would not give one verse of the Sermon on the Mount away for twenty epic poems like the Mahabharata, nor exchange the golden rule for twenty new Upanishads."

It may be mentioned in conclusion that some propose to exalt the moral teachings of Jesus by saying that for them no further religion is necessary. They will live by the Sermon on the Mount alone. But he who spoke that great and inspiring discourse gave many other teachings, ethical and spiritual. Were they superfluous? Shall we be really honoring him, or acting wisely and safely for ourselves, if we presume to select one discourse of his and treat all the rest of his teaching and his work as unnecessary and useless?

Besides, who *does* really live up to the Sermon on the Mount? Who can afford to slight the religion of Jesus, upon the assumption of fully conforming to his ethical instructions? To end as we began. He gave ethical and religious teachings together— he stands as not merely a teacher, but a Saviour. Others have taught well and helpfully, though not in a way comparable to his teaching, as to how we ought to live ; he alone can also give the spiritual help we need in order actually to live as his teachings require.

III.

The Supernatural Works of Jesus.

THE SUPERNATURAL WORKS OF JESUS.

PROFESSOR Huxley, in his "Life of David Hume" and in some recent magazine articles, admits that Hume's once celebrated position in regard to miracles cannot be maintained. Hume held that from the nature of the case, no amount of testimony can establish a miraculous event. Huxley prefers to say that alleged miraculous events require "evidence of a cogency proportionate to their departure from probability." To this, as a general principle, we should all readily agree. The testimony for a miracle must be exceedingly strong and clear. Tell me that a man who died in Washington last week has come to life, and if the matter seemed worthy of attention I should scrutinize the evidence narrowly and patiently, and engage others to do likewise with the most earnest and unwearied effort, before I could think of admitting that the alleged occurrence is real.

But in the case of Christ's miracles this need of immensely strong evidence is in a great degree offset by the fact that the miracles stand in immediate and inseparable connection with his perfect character and his peerless teachings. We have tried on former occasions to attain some conception of the Saviour's personal character, and of his exalted ethical instruction. Now in the records these are inextricably interwoven with his supernatural works. Tear out all the supernatural elements from the gospels, and the remainder will be no history at all, but a mass of shattered and broken matters worse than the ruins of so many noble buildings which the other day I left shapely and useful in the city where I dwell. Jesus himself speaks of his miracles as real. In several instances he promises beforehand, as in regard to Lazarus, and especially in regard to his own resurrection. In other cases he points back to his past miraculous work. Take the gospels as they stand, in all their beauty and simplicity, their pathos and power, and if Jesus of Nazareth did not perform supernatural works, he many times spoke falsely. The very suggestion is painful, even to many who altogether deny the supernatural. But whatever efforts may be made to evade it, the alternative faces us squarely. Either he who spake as never man spake, and in whose character no criticism can discern a fault, who shines as clear and sweet as the very morning star of humanity, either he did perform supernatural works or he spoke falsely. It might be possible that in some cases bystanders should be mistaken ; but he himself could not be mistaken. Thus then there is a highly important difference between the common run of alleged miracles, ancient or modern, and the miracles of Jesus Christ. And I am not reasoning in a circle—not proving the person by the miracles and the miracles by the person ; but they stand like the opposite parts of an arch, upholding each other, and both together upholding all that rests upon them, even the divinity of Christ's mission, and the truth of all his personal claims.

Moreover, when we survey the supernatural works ascribed in the New Testament to Jesus Christ, we find them to differ very widely as to their intrinsic character from many alleged miracles. They are all beneficent, ministering to human need, relieving human distress. " He went about doing men good." The one or two cases in which his miracles seemed not beneficent are of the very slightest importance and could be easily accounted for. Again, the miraculous healing of diseases on the part of Jesus cannot be explained by the *faith* of those concerned. He usually required faith in the applicants, and probably a good many persons at the present time have an uneasy feeling that this resembles what is now popularly called faith-cure, and that perhaps it might be explained by the mere natural influence of awakened expectation and confidence. But the Saviour healed in various instances where the sufferer was at a distance, and only the friends making the application had faith. He raised the widow's son at Nain without any request or expectation. He rose himself from the dead when his followers were not at all expecting it. He wrought miracles upon inanimate nature, the winds and the waters, and the food which he multiplied. So we cannot explain the healings by the mere natural effect of faith. Why then, it may be asked, did he so generally condition his miraculous healings upon faith? The answer seems to be, that he was always wishing to make bodily healing the occasion of spiritual benefit, and for this it was indispensable that they should have faith in him and his teachings. We can also see that his miracles were dignified, and worthy to be associated with a revelation from God. These superhuman events were the sign-manual of the Most High, given to authenticate messages sent forth from the headquarters of the universe. There is an unspeakable difference between alleged miracles sometimes trivial in themselves, and having no connection with divine revelation, and the miracles of Jesus Christ. To confound them as some objectors do, to place them all on the same footing, is to commit a profound and far-reaching error. The Saviour gave no encouragement to those who would value miracles for their own sake. He never wrought a miracle when it was demanded. Rebukingly he said, " Except ye see signs and wonders, ye will not believe." What he offered them was high spiritual and moral instruction, to be prized on its own merits, and at the same time given by one having a divine mission, one of whom Nicodemus the Sanhedrist said, for himself and others, " We know that thou hast come from God as a teacher, for no man can do these signs which thou doest, except God be with him." He did not wish to be heeded simply because of the supernatural works. Yet he distinctly and repeatedly appealed to these as attestation " The works that I do in my Father's name, they bear witness of me." " But that ye may know that the Son of man hath power on earth to forgive sins—he said to the paralytic, Arise and walk." And so he bade John's messengers carry back word that they found him healing the blind, raising the dead, and preaching good news to the poor. Thus we see that he gave no warrant for over-valuation of the miraculous, nor yet for under-valuing and neglecting it.

But how about the evidence that Jesus of Nazareth really did perform supernatural works? This is a matter upon which great stress is naturally laid by thoughtful inquirers, and which deserves the most earnest consideration.

Attempts are made in various ways to cut the matter short. Some claim that theological writers and all defenders of orthodox Christianity are constrained by hopeless prejudice, or by the necessities of their intellectual or their temporal position, to take the views they hold, and that only skeptical or agnostic writers are unprejudiced seekers after truth. Well, we human beings are all subject to prejudice, all liable to be constrained by the logical limitations of any undertaking whatsoever. They who wish to judge wisely must recognize this as a difficulty attending all human investigation. I do not at all deny that the danger exists for those who advocate the truth of Christianity as a supernatural revelation; but how strange it is for men who oppose Christianity to imagine themselves exempt from this danger. These men are compelled to explain away the Christian evidences, or else they must admit that Christianity is true; and they will feel this admission to be important just in proportion as they are men of earnest soul. For here Christianity is, in the world—often grievously corrupted, to be sure, taken by Constantine and others as a plank in their political platform, often held as the mere maid-servant of government, sometimes honey-combed with errors, encompassed with hypocrisies, and yet what a power through all the centuries; how inseparably and influentially associated with the best civilization! Now the Christ of the gospels accounts for Christianity. It rests its strongest claim upon his resurrection. And the evidence of his resurrection is immediately associated with his personal character and his noble teachings. The objectors, just in proportion as they have moral earnestness, are absolutely compelled to invalidate the evidence. They are not at all impartial nor disinterested. It is just as necessary for their intellectual and moral position to assail the evidences of Christianity as for others to maintain them.

"Well then," some one might be tempted to say, "since both sides are liable to be prejudiced and warped in judgment, we cannot hope to reach any satisfactory conclusion on the questions involved." That view of the matter, if consistently carried out, would lead us to doubt everything, since human infirmity may attach, in some way or other, to every exercise of the human faculties. But we cannot doubt everything. Some things must be true. In other directions we do rely on our faculties; why so ready just here to decry them? We must all earnestly endeavor, whichsoever side we assume with regard to any great question, to escape the dominion of prejudice and to see things as they are. And we must remember that it is the cheapest and most

facile, and perhaps the most blinding of all prejudices, to take for granted that other men are prejudiced, and we alone are exempt.

Moreover, everybody knows that a skilful lawyer,
who has a case to make out, can of course give
some plausibility to his contention, and cast some
suspicion upon opposing testimony and argument.
One who is very ingenious may temporarily per-
plex many of his hearers in regard to a sufficiently
clear case. Now the methods which some skeptical
writers employ in casting a cloud of doubt about the
evidences as to the character, teachings and supernatural works of Jesus, could be made just as effect-
ive in regard to many of the best known persons
and events of history. This has been illustrated
many times, notably by Archbishop Whately in his
taking brochure, "Historic Doubts Concerning Napoleon Bonaparte." I knew of a University student
who read this work, and said with every appearance
of sincerity that he very much questioned whether
such a man as Napoleon Bonaparte ever lived. An
interesting example is also given by Henry Rogers
in a chapter of his work entitled "The Eclipse of
Faith."

Another short method of ending the question as-
serts that "nothing is certain but what is demonstrated or demonstrable." Then a man can never
be certain that his wife loves him, or that his de-
parted mother did. Then a man cannot be certain
as to any historical occurrence, or any current
events that lie beyond his own observation, and
even our senses are quite as apt to err as our mental faculties. Then a man cannot be certain that

anything is right, or any other thing is wrong. Human life rests mainly upon practical certainties, accompanied by other matters of reasonable probability, and not exclusively or chiefly upon things demonstrated or demonstrable.*

Another class of objectors end the matter by saying that such miracles are impossible, if not theoretically impossible, yet practically and inevitably incredible. They simply cannot believe in any such interruption as they think a miracle involves in the uniform action of physical forces according to those beautiful fixed laws, about which we have been learning so much and which we ought all not only to admire with delight, but to respect and obey. But if this is a reason for summarily rejecting the possibility of miracles, that it involves such a change in the uniformity of natural action, one thing will certainly follow : The person who thus maintains will be

* It frequently happens that a young man just grown is rather skeptical about the truth of Christianity, but after some years these doubts have disappeared, without any obvious cause. The explanation is commonly this. When his mind first expanded to comprehend things, and to discriminate sharply, he craved absolute certitude about everything. But entering the various practical relations and pursuits of life, he becomes accustomed to decide important questions of duty and interest upon a mere practical centainty, or even upon fairly probable grounds, and thus he learns by degrees in the school of life a lesscn which Butler's "Analogy" has enabled some other young men to anticipate, that in many of our most important affairs " probability is the law of life." What a pity when a young man takes such early questionings as an excuse for falling into habits of immorality, or assumes a position of antagonism to Christianity, or habitually neglects its instructions and influences, so as to become disqualified for profiting by these important lessons of life's experience.

utterly inconsistent if he does not also hold that creation is an impossible conception. If one cannot believe that a superior power has ever caused physical forces to act otherwise than according to the observed uniformity, then how can he believe that these ever went through the unspeakable change of passing out of non-existence into existence? Say that miracles are essentially incredible, and how can you consistently be a Theist? Surely the Creator of these grand physical forces, who caused them to work according to these beautiful laws, surely he can interpose his higher force to control them into some unwonted action, without violating their essential nature or disturbing the harmony of the universe he created. Some, alas! accept the alternative, and say that they cannot believe in creation or a Creator. And the popular fashion at present is to call themselves Agnostics. They do not care to maintain that there is no God, and no future life for mankind; they simply do not know. Now and then one says this seriously and therefore of necessity sadly, and such persons deserve respect and consideration. But others seem to say it with easy indifference or even with arrogance. They do not know, nor care. Or they do not know, and feel proud of the recognized ignorance, and liken themselves to Socrates. Some people might remember our political Agnostics, the "Know-Nothings" of 35 years ago, and how short a time that "fad" lasted. Mr. Spurgeon remarks that this boasted name Agnostic means the same thing as ignoramus.

But it is more common at the present day to impeach the contemporary testimony to the supernat-

ural works of Jesus on the ground that the witnesses were predisposed to believe in miracles.
Suppose we state this baldly. If men are willing
to believe in miracles, their testimony as to the
occurrence of miracles must be rejected ; only men
who begin by rejecting miracles can be believed on
that subject. John Stuart Mill says that the com-
monest of all fallacies is begging the question. I
know of course that the unbelieving critic would wish
to *state* the matter otherwise. He would say, If
men strongly incline to believe in miracles their
testimony on that subject must be taken with
reserve and discount, though they be quite credible
on other subjects. Very well, only remember that
the witnesses to the Christian miracles have also
presented us the character of Christ and his ethical
teachings. But on the other hand, if men instan-
taneously reject a miracle whenever presented to
their mind, then their *judgment* on that question is
subject to a like discount. Those who hold that
miracles are practically impossible, are they good
judges of the testimony to a miracle ? Those who
follow Matthew Arnold in one of his favorite neat
phrases, and oracularly say that "miracles simply
do not happen," are they good judges ? Those who
admit that the question of miracles is a question of
evidence, but when asked to consider the evidence
for any particular miracle, obviously reject the
miracle in advance, and investigate the evidence
with a manifest and exclusive view to weaken it, are
they good judges ?

There are of course various kinds of testimony,
and each requires a certain training, that we may

with critical care and sound judgment determine its value. The great facts and principles of modern astronomy have had to work their way into general reception through immense opposition, not only from the ignorant masses of mankind, who would not believe what seemed to contradict their senses, but from many cultivated men, whose mental training had been exclusively on other sides, so that most of them could not appreciate the testimony of astronomical experts, and some gravely doubted whether the Integral Calculus was not a mere work of imagination, and Celestial Mechanics a figment of fancy. In like manner, a lack of qualification to appreciate the evidence has caused many to be very slow in accepting the best attested results of geology, or of biology, or of sociology. But the same thing is true of some admirable adepts in physical observation, some eminent specialists in one department or another of physical science, when called to judge of historical.evidence. A long-continued exclusive mental devotion to facts and methods óf quite a different kind has made it as difficult for them to estimate rightly the evidence of some great historical event as the classes of persons previously described have found it to judge rightly concerning the results of physical science. The fact is, that knowledge has become so widely developed, and specialized into so many distinct lines of investigation, and each of these pushed into such a multiplication of facts and inquiries, awakening such eagerness of effort to go farther still, as to involve all of us who are earnestly devoted to the pursuit of knowledge in great peril of becoming one-sided in

our aevelopment, and correspondingly ill-qualified
to judge concerning the offered results of investigation in departments quite unlike our own. I am
often grieved, aud sometimes angry, to see theolo-
gians and preachers undertaking to pass judgment
upon any and every question in the exact sciences,
and appearing to think that their views on these
subjects carry the authority which attaches to the
religious and moral lessons they draw from revelation. Shall I then think it wise for men who have
given their whole lives to matters of physical
observation and mathematics, and in those directions have gained deserved reputation, to take it for
granted that they are equally qualified to pass
judgment off-hand upon questions of general philosophy, or upon the validity of historical testimony? Yet not more ready are some preachers to
settle authoritatively in a single sermon the most
difficult questions as to evolution, than are some
sensation preachers of physical science to settle in a
fugitive essay the largest questions of religious history and belief, really seeming to imagine that their
views of any and all subjects are entitled to as much
respect as men justly pay to the results of their
life-long devotion in their own lines of investigation.
In this respect we are all in danger of error. And
what shall be the remedy for this tendency to growing narrowness of view and one-sidedness of judgment? Just in proportion as knowledge is becoming more specialized it seems increasingly important that a man's early training, what we call in
the technical sense his education, should not be exclusively special, but so far as possible general and

symmetrical. And then as we push out into our several lines of busy investigation, we should try through life to keep in sight and in hail of all our fellow investigators on whatsoever other lines across the broad and busy fields of inquiry. Mr. Darwin, to whom we are all so much indebted, stated, toward the close of his life, that he had lost all relish for poetry. Was not that a pity and really a blunder? I remember a few years since to have asked in a circle of some twenty cultivated gentlemen, that each would tell who was his favorite poet. Even a dear lover of poetry might be at a loss to make instant reply, but it was amusing to see how some eminent judges and other lawyers, some highly-intelligent and well-read bankers and merchants, would take on a far-away look at the very idea of having any favorite poet at all. Now ought not all of us in our several specialties of investigation or of practical activity to keep at least in general sympathy with all the other great departments of knowledge and reflection and living interest? Even if this should restrict somewhat a man's acquaintance with the actual and possible knowledge pertaining to his specialty, would it not more than compensate by giving a sounder judgment and a healthier mental action, even in regard to his own proper pursuits?

When we turn to examine the evidence that Jesus wrought supernatural works, we find one of these standing out in singular prominence, namely his own resurrection. He is recorded as having repeatedly predicted to his disciples that he would be killed and would rise again after three days. Let us attentively consider, so far as can be done in a short time, the evidence that this predicted resurrection actually occurred. I trust you will bear me witness that throughout these lectures I have tried to avoid extravagance of language and vehemence of assertion, have tried to speak soberly, in words duly weighed. It is to my mind only an apparent departure from this course to make the following statement: If I do not know that Jesus of Nazareth rose from the dead, then I know nothing in the history of mankind. If the evidence, when fully examined with a calm willingness to be convinced, does not in this case warrant a practical certainty, then there is no adequate evidence of any historical event. Let us rapidly look at the principal testimonies, remembering that such a view must necessarily be quite incomplete.

No person whatever, so far as I know, now questions that the Apostle Paul wrote the Epistles to the Corinthians, the Galatians and the Romans. There is, in fact, equally good reason to believe that he wrote other Epistles, but let that pass for the present. In the latter part of Paul's life we reach firm ground as to the dates, because Roman history tells when Festus succeeded Felix as procurator of Palestine. We thus determine that First Corinthians was written A. D. 57. Now the death of Christ cannot have been earlier than A. D. 30. So the time which had elapsed when Paul wrote this Epistle was at most 27 years, just the time from the battle of Gettysburg to the present day. Take any intelligent man among us, who has reached middle age, and consider how near to him seem the events of that great war, how clear and sure is his recollection of them. Well, in the fifteenth chapter of First Corinthians, that wonderful passage which has invested so many Christian funerals with immortal hope and unspeakable consolation, Paul declares that Christ was raised on the third day, that he appeared to Cephas and James, twice to the Twelve, and once to above five hundred brethren at once, the greater part of whom he declares to be still living. Nothing could be more explicitly asserted. And it would have been folly to make the assertion, in the face of so many skeptical and inquisitive Greeks, and so many hostile Jews in constant connection with Palestine, and the height of folly to build upon this asserted resurrection of Christ, his entire argument for a Christian doctrine which some of the Church at Corinth were explicitly denying, if there had been the least doubt that these numerous surviving witnesses existed and could be found. Paul risks his own veracity and all his influence as an Apostle, risks the entire truth of Christianity, upon the one point. " If Christ hath not been raised, then is our preaching vain, your faith also is vain." He builds everything upon this great fact. Several times in Second Corinthians also he speaks of the Lord Jesus as raised from the dead ; also in Galatians, and again and again in the great Epistle to the Romans, written a few months after those to the Corinthians. Here he again makes the fact of Christ's resurrection the starting point for proofs concerning him and his mission and work, and he declares that to believe that God raised Jesus from

the dead is the faith of the gospel, carrying everything with it. In his earlier epistles to the Thessalonians, written as much as five years before Corinthians, he not only speaks of Jesus as raised from
the dead, but argues from that fact. "If we believe that Jesus died and rose again, even so them
also that are fallen asleep in Jesus will God bring
with him." The same fact is also asserted in his
later epistles, as Colossians, Ephesians, Timothy.
And besides formal assertions, he often speaks of it
as a matter of course, recognized by all.

Now Paul the Apostle was assuredly no ordinary
man. It does not require life-long study such as I
have given to his history and writings to perceive
that he was a man of powerful intellect, immense
force of character, unimpeachable sincerity, and—a
matter which will grow upon one when his attention
has been turned to it—a man of singular common
sense. We know that he was at first utterly opposed to the faith of the Christians, denying, de-
spising, persecuting with all the passionate ardor of
his soul, and sincerely believing that in all this he
was doing his duty. He had been the foremost
student in the leading College at Jerusalem ; the
highest prizes of attainment, distinction and power
that pertained to his country and his calling were
easily within the reach of his ardent and ambitious
soul. When he turned from all this to join the few
thousands of the sect which he had persecuted and
seemed likely to crush, and which had nothing
worldly to offer, it was assuredly a notable event,
one which has profoundly impressed itself upon
thoughtful minds through all the ages. Let me

tell an old story. In the middle of the last century
an Englishman, Lord Lyttelton, and his friend Gil-
bert West, a brother of the great painter, concerted
together, being unbelievers in the Bible as a revelation, that each should select some Bible topic and
after thorough study prepare a small treatise ˉupon
it, for the purpose of showing the absurdity of the
Christian claims. West chose the Resurrection of
Christ, and Lyttelton the Conversion of Paul.
When they met some time afterwards each expected to surprise and grieve the other by confess-
ing that his researches had led him to believe in
Christianity and the Bible, and each published a short
treatise on the subject to that effect. West's has
been superseded by more vigorous discussions.
But Lord Lyttelton's little work, " Observations on
the Conversion of St. Paul," is still current. Gruff
old Dr. Johnson called it " a treatise to which in-
fidelity has never been able to fabricate a specious
answer." Lyttelton has most impressively argued
that Paul's conversion cannot be explained as due
to imposture or fanaticism ; and his conversion oc
curred only a few years after Christ's departure.
This highly intelligent and strongly prejudiced man
had every opportunity of knowing the facts, and
every inducement to examine them with care, and
he became fully convinced that Jesus of Nazareth
had risen from the dead, and in that conviction
lived and labored, suffered and died. Keim, in his
" Jesus of Nazara," a work of great compass and of
unsurpassed learning and ability, is sufficiently
skeptical and destructive as a critic, for he rejects
the fourth gospel, and cuts away from the others

whatever he pleases; yet Keim declares, "Paul's help supplies the whole question with its fixed point, its Archimedean fulcrum; and the universal conviction of earliest Christendom acquires the historical basis which gives it certainty and clothes it with flesh and blood. This universal conviction was of itself able to stand against a doubt of its truth; but in the face of the testimony of Paul, the force of such a doubt is doubly lost." Keim held that historical science is bound within the limits of "material perception and the natural order of the world." With this definition he of course thought that there can be no *scientific* proof of Christ's resurrection. But he insists that Christian faith in that resurrection "is not only beyond the reach of refutation, since science is compelled to leave the mystery of the final events of Jesus' career unsolved without weakening the foundations of faith by a single comment; but it completes and illumines what to science remained an obscure point and a vexatious limitation of its knowledge." And where is the propriety of thus limiting historical science to the range of material perception, and the sphere of natural order? If any supernatural events have really occurred, they are a part of the facts of history, and can not be omitted from the view of a just historical science. As well justify the Ptolemaic astronomy, which held that the heavens revolve round the earth, and being unable to account for the changing position of certain bright stars, simply called them "wanderers," planets. Thus likewise some produce very symmetrical systems of theology, by omitting inconvenient facts of revela-

tion or of consciousness. In excluding the supernatural from history by his very definition, Keim
makes, I think, an arbitrary assumption. But all
the more remarkable and significant is the practical conclusion he so strongly announced as to the
fact of Christ's resurrection.

Now remember that the testimony of Paul's contemporary letters, accompanied by his remarkable
conversion and his noble character and career,
though many regard it as in itself ample evidence,
by no means stands alone. Peter also speaks of
the Saviour's resurrection in his first epistle, speaks
of it as a matter of course, recognized by all his
readers, just as Paul had often done. And Peter
repeatedly makes strong statements to the same
effect in his speeches recorded in the Acts of the
Apostles. This book of Acts was forty years ago
vehemently assailed by Baur, and the once famous
Tübingen school which he founded, for whom it
was necessary to throw the book overboard because
forsooth it conflicted with their theory. Baur held
that the conflict between Paul and certain Jewish
Christians, who insisted that all Gentile converts
ought to be circumcised and live as Jews, and who
claimed Peter and James as their leaders and declared
Paul to be no apostle, was really a conflict between
the apostles themselves; that Paul and his followers
on the one hand, and Peter and James with their
followers on the other hand, were bitterly hostile.
Baur thought he could find proof of this in the second
chapter of Galatians especially, and also to some
extent in Romans and in First and Second Corinthians. He could not discern any semblance of

such proof in the other epistles of Paul, and it was
for this reason, and so far as I can see for this reason alone, that he declared Corinthians, Galatians
and Romans to be the only genuine epistles of Paul.
This statement or expression was taken up by
second-hand organs of skeptical opinion, and has
continued fashionable to the present time.   We are
perfectly at liberty to show that these four epistles
which all acknowledge to be genuine contain ample proof of the resurrection of Christ, and also contain all the leading facts as to his person and work,
and the leading doctrines of the Christian system.
But there is positively no reason, apart from Baur's
theory, for refusing to recognize Thessalonians and
Philippians, which so closely resemble the four
above-mentioned.   Nor is there any good reason for
rejecting Colossians and Ephesians, or Titus and
Timothy.   For, while these differ from the earlier
groups in their leading topics, they are simply the
topics suggested by the rise of new errors to be com-
bated.   And while the style of these later groups of
epistles is unlike that of the earlier, it is only such a
change of style as will always be observable in a first-
rate writer when his subjects change—a fact which
Bishop Westcott once happily expressed in a private letter by borrowing a phrase from the higher
mathematics and saying that " style is a function of
the subject as well as of the author."   Holding then
that Paul was really at enmity with Peter and James,
as supposed to be shown by Galatians, and finding
that the book of Acts represents these apostles as
repeatedly consulting together and entirely harmonious, Baur coolly declared that the book of Acts

was spurious; that it was written at a later period
when the Paul party had triumphed, for the purpose
of concealing the original conflict. But all this Tübingen theory, which once attracted immense attention and threatened to darken the whole heavens,
has blown away, leaving scarce a rack behind.
Bishop Lightfoot, Dr. Fisher of Yale and others, as
well as many in Germany, conclusively showed that
the second chapter of Galatians not only fails to
confirm the theory, but actually disproves it. There
is to-day no historical ground to maintain that Paul
was arrayed against the other apostles; no reason to
question the account given in the book of Acts,
that while some Judaizers claiming Peter and
James as their leaders, were hostile to Paul, there
was no hostility nor disagreement between the
apostles themselves. And if any still assert the
contrary, they belong to that class of English and
American writers who set forth as surprising novel-
ties, or as the best results of recent inquiry, German
theories long ago dead and buried in their native
land. Whether some popular and very noisy theories now prevalent as to the Old Testament will in
like manner pass away, is not for me to predict.
But we hear scarcely anything now against the
authenticity of the book of Acts, much of it so evidently the work of an eye-witness, and all giving
proof of careful research and remarkable accuracy.
Its accuracy at various points has been curiously
confirmed by recent excavations in Cyprus and
Ephesus, and by researches concerning the account
of Paul's voyage and shipwreck. Renan, who is
surely skeptical enough for ordinary demands, has

stated that there is little or no reason to question
that the third gospel and the book of Acts, which are
evidently from the same hand, are the works of
Luke, a companion of the Apostle Paul.

Now this book of Acts, as already said; abounds in
passing references as well as express assertions concerning the resurrection of Christ.   And Part I. of
the same work on the Beginnings of Christianity,
or what we call the Gospel according to Luke, gives
details of that wonderful event, and touchingly
narrates appearances of the risen Lord to some of
his followers.

This reminds us that each of the four gospels not
only states but describes with more or less detail,
the Saviour's resurrection, and some of his subse-
quent appearances.   It is a strange thing to find
some objectors still repeating that these four accounts are contradictory in their details, and therefore not trustworthy.   One charitably supposes
that they must be merely repeating without personal investigation what used to be said when the so-
called " discrepancies " of the gospels were the
stock in trade of certain critical assailants.   Over
and over again it has been shown, and I think conclusively shown, that here and elsewhere the difference in details of the parallel narratives in the gospels must really strengthen their credibility.   Persons who have often attended upon trials in court,
to say nothing of these who have studied legal
treatises on evidence, are well aware that when
several witnesses in narrating a series of events
agree as to the main facts, their united testimony
is only strengthened and confirmed by disagree-

ment in minor details, even if occasionally we do not quite see how some slight point of disagreement is to be explained. If they coincided in every minute particular, we should know the witnesses had put their heads together, and should not believe them at all. The application of this to the gospels has for a good many years been so well recognized by most of those who really examine the matter, that we find the allegation of contradiction in the gospel narratives now rarely made except by second-hand writers, who borrow from older works. I have sometimes half imagined that the change in Germany of late years is partly due to the intro-duction, after 1848, of trial by jury. I wonder whether those magnificent devotees to study who lead the world in scholarly attainment, have per-haps mixed enough with the active world, or looked in enough upon the courts of justice, to get some inkling of the laws of evidence in respect to this matter. However that may be, the change is doubtless mainly due to the usual oscillations of speculation and inquiry. Instead of now troubling themselves with points of disagreement in the gospels, many German critics, and some in other countries, are greatly exercised to account for the *agreement*. Va-rious theories have been proposed to explain the fact that considerable portions of Matthew, Mark and Luke contain not only the same substantial matter, but often quite similar phraseology. Thus some hold that Matthew and Luke drew from Mark; others that Mark and Luke drew from Matthew; yet others that all three drew from some pre-existing document or documents which soon perished. A view which I should prefer, if compelled to choose, is that the apostles in their oral teaching gradually fell into a certain cycle of selected sayings and actions of their Master; and that we can thus account for the agreement at many points. Many of us, however, have really no theory to offer as to the agreement of the three gospels, and are patiently waiting to see if any valuable results will come from the tossing to and fro of ingenious speculations and elaborate inquiries.

But what proof have we that the gospels are of apostolic origin? For any thorough examination of this question, most persons have to rely on those who make it a specialty. We need not be surprised at such a necessity. We have to rely on lawyers as to the titles to our property, on physicians to determine our diseases and prescribe remedies, and on druggists to prepare the medicine. Any one of these may err and ruin us, but we have to make the best selection in our power, and take the consequences. Why wonder that a similar situation exists as to determining the external proof for the canon of Scripture? As regards the *internal* evidences, every thoughtful reader can largely judge for himself. And if only men would thoughtfully read the gospels, coming near in historical imagination to the person they exhibit, and listening with simple candor to his words of wisdom and love, many who are skeptical now would feel all that is best in them drawn toward him in living sympathy and devotion. The Scriptures in general, and the four gospels in particular, carry credentials of their own on every page.

In respect then to the external evidence, I shall say but little. Yet it may be mentioned that interesting progress has been made within a few years. The Tübingen school used to maintain that the fourth gospel was not written till after the middle of the second century. Their really able and learned efforts to maintain this theory have led to thoroughgoing investigation, and the date of this gospel's historically ascertained existence has been pushed back farther and farther, until one of the representatives of the school admitted that it existed as early as A. D. 120, which is only some twenty-five years later than the ordinarily assigned date of its composition. The late Professor Ezra Abbot of Harvard, probably the foremost American scholar in this particular department, undertook some years ago to investigate the origin of the fourth gospel, with a pre-disposition (as he afterward avowed) to regard it as decidedly post-apostolic. Going into the matter with his usual thoroughness and patience, he reached the opposite conclusion, and published an elaborate essay to prove that the fourth gospel was written by the Apostle John. This work, along with various discussions in Germany and England, must in my judgment be regarded as practically settling that question. The Tübingen school has broken down here as completely as with reference to the book of Acts; and as often occurs in every department of human inquiry, patient examination has at length overtaken and overcome the most fleet-footed and shrill-voiced hypothesis.

We have long known from ample historical evidence that our four gospels were unhesitatingly received in every section of the Christian world in the latter part of the second century. This is fully shown by the statements of Irenæus, Clement of Alexandria and Tertullian, by the use of the four gospels in the two Egyptian versions, in the Old Latin version or versions, and in the Old Syriac version, which was discovered some thirty years ago. Quite recently we have regained the long-lost Diatessaron of Tatian, the earliest known Harmony of the gospels, prepared soon after the middle of the second century; and it makes at once manifest the fact that Tatian's four gospels were ours. Important light has also been thrown upon the numerous citations from the gospels in the works of Justin Martyr, now believed by many to have been written earlier than A. D. 150. Justin's quotations, though evidently the same in substance with passages in our gospels, differ widely in the expressions employed and often confound or mingle similar passages ; and sometimes he adds curious statements of things said or done which must have been traditional. Accordingly some objectors have earnestly contended that his gospels must have been different from ours, though they have found it hard to account for the sudden disappearance of every vestige of these supposed earlier writings. Now it has long been observed, as is shown in Dr. Gildersleeve's excellent edition of Justin's Apologies, that he quotes with great looseness from the Septuagint also, and greatly alters the phraseology of favorite passages in Plato and Xenophon which must have been thoroughly familiar to the philosophic emperors he addressed. We see that his memory was quite inaccurate as to details, though he scarcely ever misrepresents the substance. Even in our day of convenient printed editions and concordances, inexact quotation of Scripture is quite frequent. But still, Justin's additional statements drawn from tradition were not accounted for. Now the epoch-making labors of Westcott and Hort concerning the Greek text of the New Testament have shown that Justin habitually used what is technically called the "Western" type of text, which was very corrupt and had various additions from tradition, and was widely diffused before the middle of the second century; and existing documents of that "Western" text present in one case or another the very additions which Justin gives. So there is no longer any particle of reason to think that he had different gospels; he simply used our gospels in the "Western" text. If one is startled at the idea that a very corrupt text of the gospels was used in many quarters before the middle of the second century, a little reflection will show in this fact a clear and strong proof that the gospels had been long in existence and widely received—an argument which Tischendorf already wrought out in his little work on the "Origin of the Gospels."

The historical existence of the gospels of Matthew and Mark is pushed still further back by well-known statements of Papias, written about A. D. 130 to 140; and the gospel of Matthew is quoted as Scripture in the so-called Epistle of Barnabas, which must have been written very early in the century. The recently discovered and already famous little treatise entitled "Teaching of the

Apostles," upon which Professor Rendel Harris and many others have labored, certainly belongs to the second century, and is by most writers referred to the beginning of the century; and it contains numerous quotations from Matthew and Luke. There are also gospel quotations in the Epistles of Ignatius, and in the Epistle of Clement of Rome, which was written before the end of the first century, the earliest extant Christian writing after the New Testament.

On the historical evidence thus briefly stated I may remark two things. We find references to the gospels wherever we could possibly expect to find them, considering the paucity of early Christian literature, and the character and design of the extant writings. The other remark is, that the Christians of the first centuries had much more copious information than they have transmitted to us, and however uncritical they may seem to us in some respects, were extremely solicitous about the ascertainment and recognition of apostolic writings.

Now let us return to the resurrection of Jesus. Besides the great and varied testimony of Paul, which many careful enquirers have regarded as in itself amply sufficient, besides the testimony of Peter in his epistles and the numerous and implied statements in the book of Acts, we have the four gospels, giving their four independent narratives, with multiplied details, of the resurrection of Christ. Even if Matthew, Mark, and Luke be supposed to have drawn some statements from a pre-existing document, or from a common cycle of oral instruction, they separately adopt these statements and thus

separately endorse them. I wish there was time to
dwell on the beautifully diversified and yet not
really conflicting details with which the four
gospels describe the Lord's resurrection ; and on
the varied, suggestive, and deeply impressive appearances after the resurrection which one or another
of them records. I should like to present, as I have
tried to do elsewhere in print, some obvious con-
siderations, which go to account for his appearing
to believers only, as for example that any public
appearance would have stirred the Jewish multitude into fanatical frenzy, and with their notions
concerning the Messiah, into mad revolution, and
would likely enough have aroused the Jewish
rulers into some scheme of putting him to death
again, as they had muttered a purpose of doing with
Lazarus.

Those who are determined not to accept the
various and multiplied evidence of the Saviour's
resurrection must of course suggest some explanation of the unquestionable belief in it among the
first Christians. Nobody now calls the story an
imposture ; all that passed away with such writers
as Tom Paine. Some imagine that the Saviour
had not really died. But remember Pilate's special inquiry and the official examination, remember the soldier's spear, upon which special stress is
laid by the apostolic eye-witness who wrote the
fourth gospel, remember the Saviour's personal
veracity in predicting that he would die and in
saying afterwards that he had died and risen again,
remember the agreement with prophecies, which
were not understood by the apostles in advance,

but became clear afterwards. Some say that certain followers of Jesus saw mere visions of him and pursuaded the rest that these were real appearances. Renan actually imagines that the whole belief came from Mary Magdalene, whom he calls " a hallucinated woman," and who led the apostles and above five hundred persons, and finally all Christians, to believe that the Saviour had appeared to her alive. Yet in the *records* the apostles and others seem to us passing *slow* to believe, almost rudely repelling the first testimonies of the women, and convinced only when Jesus appeared in the midst of their circle, inviting examination of his person, and giving irrefragable proof that here was no vision, but a body with flesh and bones, and bearing the marks of crucifixion. As was long ago said, " they doubted, that we might not doubt." And if others are imagined to have presently shared the visions and thought them actual appearances, why were these visions so few, so brief and orderly and sober, and why did they so early cease ? How can those who have given us the character and teachings of Jesus, before which all the world stands in admiration, and who were so despairing and slow of belief, have been convinced by mere dreams ? The Apostle Paul says he had several visions, giving him divine direction and encouragement at turning-points of his ministry, but he expressly distinguishes from these the appearance which occasioned his conversion, saying that it occurred at midday, while he was journeying, and that Jesus spoke to him out of heaven, and that he saw Jesus Christ the Lord.

" Oh, but it was all so long ago." Yet we must

remember that their testimony was recorded, and was confirmed by a new and permanent religious organization, and by new and significant symbols of ceremony, which have come down all the centuries parallel with the records. " But how do we know that the supernatural elements of the gospels were not added by other writers in the generation immediately following the apostolic age, from which we have so little historical information ? " I answer, What reason is there for thinking that they were so added ? The writings have unity, of character and aim, and of style and tone. Nobody would dream of cutting out large portions of such writings, without the slightest external ground, except persons who were determined beforehand to reject at all hazards whatever savors of the supernatural. And what is this but simply and flagrantly begging the question ? There is a homely story of a Scotchman who said, " I am open to conviction, but I'd like to see the mon that could convince me." Now I do not apply this to every one who questions, or hesitates to accept, the reality of our Lord's resurrection—by no means ; but only to those who without the slightest external warrant or internal opening would pluck out and relegate to a later period the supernatural elements of the gospels, and then coolly say that the genuine records of Jesus contain nothing supernatural.

It has not been possible in so brief a compass to give any adequate statement of the evidences which to my mind so conclusively show that the Founder of Christianity did actually rise from the dead, as all his first followers believed, including those who wrote the wonderful books we call the New Testament, as they attested by all manner of sacrifice and heroism, and many of them by martyr deaths.   The proofs are eminently cumulative in their character, and in many cases depend greatly on appreciation of the details.   But I am fully persuaded that whoever will read over the references to this subject in the Acts and Epistles, and the descriptions given in the four gospels, and will consider all the circumstances, and reflect upon the power which a belief in the Lord's resurrection gave to Christianity, whoever will examine the whole matter with the evidence that is open to us all, and with ordinary human willingness to be convinced, must be very profoundly impressed by the multiplied evidence ; and I see not how such a one can fail to accept that sublime fact which from the outset formed the central pillar of the Christian evidences.

When once this great supernatural work of Jesus is accepted, there is little need to argue as to the intrinsic probability or attendant circumstances of his other miracles.   If he rose from the dead, according to his own prediction, this authenticates all his teachings and all his claims.   Then indeed, as Paul wrote to the Romans, he " was born of the seed of David according to the flesh, and was declared to be the Son of God with power according to the spirit of holiness by resurrection from the dead."   For this resurrection set the seal of divine approval upon all that he claimed, and he claimed to be the Son of God.   If he rose from the dead, then his teachings, which profess to be a revelation from God, are to be so received, with all confidence and all submission. Revelation itself, however given, is necessarily supernatural; and other supernatural works accompanying a revela‑ tion may well seem to us altogether in place, acting as external credentials in harmony with its own in‑ ternal claims and adaptations. If Jesus Christ rose from the dead, then his immediate followers, to whom he promised the special mission of the di‑ vine Spirit, to bring all things to their remembrance which they had heard from him, and to guide them into all the truth, are themselves also authoritative instructors concerning him and in his name. If he rose from the dead, then we need have no difficul‑ ty in accepting whatever is clearly and surely taught in the accompanying revelation concerning his Incarnation, his Atonement, and the work of Regeneration by the Spirit whom he sent as his successor. Then also Jesus Christ authenticates for us the Old Testament. For he and his apostles have repeatedly declared the Scriptures to be from God, and to be of indestructible authority. But we know from ample Jewish and Christian evidence, that what his hearers would inevitably understand by the term Scriptures, and what he therefore must have meant, would be exactly the books which we call the Old Testament. And behold, what new views we gain as to the meaning of that wonderful collection of ancient and varied writings, the Old Testament, when it is seen how all their teachings converge toward him, and become one great History of Redemption.

But still, I can imagine some one saying, it is so hard to bring that first Christianity near to our‑

selves. It shines like a star, but it seems so distant. Christianity has indeed been by many sadly corrupted, grievously abused. But consider, every gift of genius is abused by many, every form of government has been corrupted, every dearest relation of life that ought to make us blessed may be so misused as to render us miserable. And think how much good Christianity has done, and how much more good it assuredly would do, if we who call ourselves Christians would live more faithfully according to its requirements and in the inspiration of its motives and hopes, and would more zealously carry out the departing Saviour's commission, and preach repentance and remission of sins unto all nations.

Let us remember too that believing in Jesus Christ and his religion is not like believing in some mathematical formula, or some metaphysical conclusion, or some ascertainment of general history. If Christianity be true, it is gloriously true—yea, and tremendously true. Remember furthermore ; Christianity is not only a system of ethics, or a system of doctrines, it is embodied in a *person.* Egotism is often ridiculous ; but take one step upward, and behold it is a sublime egotism when Jesus Christ says, " I am the way, and the truth, and the life. No one cometh unto the Father but through me." Through him, then, let us draw near, on him let us personally rely. It may be that differences of doctrinal conception are at present unavoidable, but why shall we not all trust and lovingly obey the personal Saviour ? Nor must we forget that to hold aloof from Christianity is not simply rejecting some creed, or system of opinion, it is rejecting Jesus Christ himself, the Son of God, the Saviour of men. Cannot each one of us say at least so much as this, " Lord, I believe, help thou mine unbelief?" Behold, he who one day said that to Jesus was heard and blessed.

DR. BROADUS'S WORK ON PREACHING.

ON THE PREPARATION AND DELIVERY OF SERMONS.

By JOHN A. BROADUS, D.D., LL.D.   Crown 8vo.   514 pages.

No other work on the same subject, published in this country, has sold so largely in so short a time, while the religious and secular press, in all parts of the country, has almost universally commended it in strong and earnest notices.

Its immediate REPUBLICATION IN LONDON, *with an Introduction by Rev. Joseph Angus, D.D., was followed by the indorsement of Bishop Ellicott, Rev. C. H. Spurgeon, and the religious periodicals, demonstrating that it met with equal favor abroad.*

The work not only meets the wants of students and young ministers, but is very suggestive and stimulating to those of maturer age. It is warmly commended to Sunday-school teachers, lay preachers and, public speakers in general. It takes unusual pains to give suggestions for the preparation and conduct of what is called extemporaneous discourse, while doing full justice to all the methods.

NOTICES OF THE WORK.

"Prepared by a very able teacher. He has had a practical knowledge of his subject, is intimately acquainted with the literature of all parts of it, and has treated the whole with devoutness, thoroughness, blended scholarship, and good sense."— *Dr. Angus*, in Preface to London edition.

"The preacher who desires to have an intelligent appreciation of the demands of his work, and of the way in which he may attain excellency in it, cannot do better than study this thoughtful and suggestive treatise."—*English Independent.*

"A book on preaching, by a master of the art. Everywhere in his book there is that intensity of earnestness which is at once the charm and characteristic of his preaching."—*Religious Herald.*

"A judicious and exhaustive treatise—destined, we think, to occupy a very prominent, if not the highest place among books on Homiletics."—*Methodist Home Journal.*

"Abounds in excellent hints, rules, and suggestions. It is very lucid in style—must do good on a large scale."—*Southern Presbyterian.*

"It bears the marks of close study, of careful deliberation, is always suggestive, breathes a good pure spirit, and has a style that is always clear and attractive."—*Lutheran and Missionary.*

"A rich mine of the best thoughts on the grandest subject." — *Raleigh Episcopal Methodist.*

"Elaborate in plan and execution, systematically arranged—we commend the volume as one of the best of its kind."—*The Advance.*

"The most complete and comprehensive work of the kind published in this country." —*Christian Intelligencer.*

"A good book ; full of instruction, rich, varied, and exhaustive."—*Princeton Review.*

"I know of no one book from which a clergyman can learn so much of the art of preaching."—*W. Sparrow, D.D., Prof. in Prot. Epis. Theol. Seminary of Va.*

"Even for the general reader it has unusual attractions. It is exceedingly readable and charmingly written."—*The World.*

"Sabbath-school superintendents and teachers will be guided, helped, and strengthened by it."—*S. School Times.*

"It abounds in suggestions which may be turned to profitable account, not only by preachers, but by lawyers, and all others who are called upon to address public audiences."—*American Lit. Gazette.*

"We have read the book with absorbing interest. Rich, deep thoughts and eminently practical suggestions abound through these pages."—*Associate Reformed Presbyterian.*

Other Solid Ground Titles

In addition to the book *Jesus of Nazareth* which you hold in your hand, Solid Ground is honored to offer many other uncovered treasure, many for the first time in more than a century:

THE CHILD AT HOME by John S.C. Abbott
THE KING'S HIGHWAY: *The 10 Commandments for the Young* by Richard Newton
THE LIFE OF JESUS CHRIST FOR THE YOUNG by Richard Newton
LET THE CANNON BLAZE AWAY by Joseph P. Thompson
THE STILL HOUR: *Communion with God in Prayer* by Austin Phelps
COLLECTED WORKS of James Henley Thornwell (4 vols.)
CALVINISM IN HISTORY *by Nathaniel S. McFetridge*
OPENING SCRIPTURE: *Hermeneutical Manual by Patrick Fairbairn*
THE ASSURANCE OF FAITH *by Louis Berkhof*
THE PASTOR IN THE SICK ROOM *by John D. Wells*
THE BUNYAN OF BROOKLYN: *Life & Sermons of I.S. Spencer*
THE NATIONAL PREACHER: *Sermons from 2nd Great Awakening*
FIRST THINGS: *First Lessons God Taught Mankind Gardiner Spring*
BIBLICAL & THEOLOGICAL STUDIES *by 1912 Faculty of Princeton*
THE POWER OF GOD UNTO SALVATION *by B.B. Warfield*
THE LORD OF GLORY *by B.B. Warfield*
A GENTLEMAN & A SCHOLAR: *Memoir of J.P. Boyce* by J. Broadus
SERMONS TO THE NATURAL MAN *by W.G.T. Shedd*
SERMONS TO THE SPIRITUAL MAN *by W.G.T. Shedd*
HOMILETICS AND PASTORAL THEOLOGY *by W.G.T. Shedd*
A PASTOR'S SKETCHES 1 & 2 *by Ichabod S. Spencer*
THE PREACHER AND HIS MODELS *by James Stalker*
IMAGO CHRISTI *by James Stalker*
A HISTORY OF PREACHING *by Edwin C. Dargan*
LECTURES ON THE HISTORY OF PREACHING *by J. A. Broadus*
THE SCOTTISH PULPIT *by William Taylor*
THE SHORTER CATECHISM ILLUSTRATED *by John Whitecross*
THE CHURCH MEMBER'S GUIDE *by John Angell James*
THE SUNDAY SCHOOL TEACHER'S GUIDE *by John A. James*
CHRIST IN SONG: *Hymns of Immanuel from All Ages* by Philip Schaff
COME YE APART: *Daily Words from the Four Gospels* by J.R. Miller
DEVOTIONAL LIFE OF THE S.S. TEACHER *by J.R. Miller*

Call us Toll Free at 1-877-666-9469
Send us an e-mail at sgcb@charter.net
Visit us on line at solid-ground-books.com

www.ingramcontent.com/pod-product-compliance
Lightning Source LLC
Chambersburg PA
CBHW030109070426
42448CB00036B/587